D1107410

PARAPSYCHOLOGY

Frontier Science of the Mind

133.8
R345p

(*Revised Second Printing*)

PARAPSYCHOLOGY,

FRONTIER SCIENCE OF THE MIND

*A Survey of the Field, the Methods, and the Facts of
ESP and PK Research*

By

J. B. RHINE *and* J. G. PRATT

*Parapsychology Laboratory
Duke University
Durham, North Carolina*

73033

CHARLES C THOMAS • PUBLISHER

Springfield • Illinois • U.S.A.

LIBRARY ST. MARY'S COLLEGE

WITHDRAWN

CHARLES C THOMAS • PUBLISHER
BANNERSTONE HOUSE
301-327 East Lawrence Avenue, Springfield, Illinois, U.S.A.

This book is protected by copyright. No part
of it may be reproduced in any manner without written permission from the publisher.

© 1957, by CHARLES C THOMAS • PUBLISHER

First Printing, 1957
Revised Second Printing, 1962

Library of Congress Catalog Card Number: 57–10999

Printed in the United States of America

Foreword

THERE ARE many indications that the time has come to provide a convenient one-volume summary of present knowledge about parapsychology. Most urgent is the need among busy professional people for a clear, concise statement of the known facts of this new field of science, just how the researches are carried on and what general advance has been made in relating the new findings to older branches of knowledge. Outstanding among the audience we have had in mind are the various professional groups connected with medicine and the psychological and social sciences and practices. This book was undertaken as a result.

There are other professional groups, too, for whom the volume was intended as a handbook of essential information on the subject: The teacher, for example, or minister or field worker in anthropology should, we believe, find it as well suited to his purpose as the psychiatrist or dermatologist or clinical psychologist. In a word, the competent, mature inquirer, whatever his professional field, should consider that the book was written for him.

Finally, these pages have been written, too, with the coming need of a college textbook in mind. Two university requests for such a text have recently been received, and with the present prospects of the growth of parapsychology, others are anticipated.

More popularly written introductory books on parapsychology have been published in recent years. The titles of most of them may be found in the literature cited in the book. Younger students and nonprofessional readers making their approach to parapsychology may find it advantageous to read one or more of these other works by way of introduction.

This book is, of course, not meant for our long-experienced fellow workers in parapsychology, nor even for the well-read highly informed student of the field who knows most of its scientific literature at firsthand. Likewise, it should not be considered as intended to answer and satisfy completely all the questions the

v

extremely skeptical reader might raise; we cannot take space for all that, especially now that it is largely of historic interest only. Those who begin here can, however, readily find the way to the supporting literature with the help of the frequent references provided.

The plan of the book is simply to state the established facts and to offer in the text references to the main publications that cover the researches concerned. Only the main references, however, are given. None but the research parapsychologist would need the rest, and he well knows how to find them himself. This book, rather, is designed to be read and consulted by those who do not already know the field but who wish, to some extent at least, to enter it with proper information at hand. Each section and sub-section is labeled, identified and indexed as clearly as possible to make the search for needed items a quick and easy one.

The essential features of method and apparatus are photo-graphically illustrated. The procedures, both methodological and evaluative, are given to an extent that should serve the purpose for all but the professional parapsychologist himself. If there are shortcomings encountered, we want to know about them for cor-rection on revision, and if information is lacking that the reader cannot himself find with the help of the available references, we will welcome direct inquiry from readers.

We are indebted to our publisher, Mr. Charles C Thomas, for the suggestion that this book should be written. Our greatest obli-gation, of course, is to our fellow-workers in parapsychology who have given us the findings these pages review. We are especially grateful to those colleagues who have helped with the manuscript: Dr. R. J. Cadoret, Dr. Louisa E. Rhine, Dr. R. H. Thouless, Dr. T. N. E. Greville, Dr. J. A. Greenwood, Mrs. Sally Feather, Mrs. Farilla David, and Mrs. Joan Walker. We have, of course, to hold ourselves responsible for whatever inadequacies the book may still reveal.

J.B.R.
J.G.P.

Parapsychology Laboratory of
Duke University
Durham, North Carolina

Contents

PART II
TESTING TECHNIQUES

Illustrations

PARAPSYCHOLOGY
Frontier Science of the Mind

PART I

Present Knowledge

Chapter 1

A Field of Science

I. Definition of the Field

THE SCIENCE of parapsychology began with the interest aroused by the reports of spontaneous human experiences and events that are familiarly known as "psychic." These puzzling phenomena have never been claimed by any of the conventional branches of science, and until comparatively recent decades they had been ignored by all but a few scientists. Yet records of such occurrences have come from peoples of all cultures and periods and, simply as reported human experiences, they would manifestly have some proper claim on the attention of science. Moreover, they raise some very distinct and important questions for experimental investigation. At this point, however, these odd types of experiences are mentioned only to help in identifying the subject matter of the new science with which this volume is concerned.

It should from the very beginning be made clear that the phenomena with which parapsychology deals are all, without exception, events of nature. In other words, the field of problems belongs entirely to *natural science*. As the next chapter will indicate, the observations and experiments are dealt with strictly in the established manner of scientific inquiry. Accordingly, whatever comes out of the investigations of this field belongs, just as in any other branch of science, to the body of organized knowledge known as natural law.

More specifically, the observations and events dealt with in parapsychology—parapsychical phenomena—are associated in some central way with *living* organisms, as distinguished from inanimate matter. To limit the area still further, this science deals only (as far as we know) with behaving organisms; not, for ex-

5

ample, with bacteria or grains of corn except as these might be involved incidentally. Thus parapsychology belongs not only in the realm of biology but it is localized in the sub-division of psychology, the science concerned with persons, personality, or personal agency within the living world.

What, then, identifies a psychical phenomenon as parapsychical? It is an occurrence that has been shown by experimental investigation to be unexplainable wholly in terms of physical principles. It is, in fact, the manifestly nonphysical character of parapsychical phenomena that for the present constitutes their only general identifying feature and marks them off from the rest of general psychology. This does not, of course, alter the fact that the data of parapsychology are natural. As a matter of fact, our concept of what is "natural" is built up out of just such discoveries of science as they are made; accordingly it goes on growing, and will continue to do so, with each added bit of knowledge. It is now clear that, contrary to some of the limiting philosophies that currently prevail, nature extends beyond the domain of purely physical law.

The distinction of these parapsychical occurrences from physics is *not*, however, an absolute one. Rather, they usually involve physical events or objects, either as stimuli or as effects. *But there is always some distinct point at which a completely physical interpretation is manifestly inadequate.* To illustrate, the direct influence of human volition on a moving object without the use of any kind of physical energy to achieve the effect would constitute a phenomenon for parapsychological study. Or again, an individual may obtain knowledge of an event occurring beyond the range of his senses and his reasoning abilities. If there should be no transfer of physical energy from the event to the individual, no sensory function could convey the knowledge and the experience would be parapsychical.

Every science necessarily begins with an area of "unknowns" with a group of interrelated phenomena that challenge explanation by the already existing sciences. At the earliest stage of a new scientific field it is usually hard to define the aggregate of the little-understood phenomena well enough for useful discussion. But parapsychology has already passed this stage, and we may

now characterize it as the branch of inquiry which deals with nonphysical personal operations or phenomena.

This definition of parapsychology, while sharp enough for practical purposes, is naturally limited to the present stage of knowledge, as indeed all terminologies must be. It is strictly the parapsychology of today, the physics of today, and the psychology of
today that must be dealt with in the working concepts of the times.
There is, thus, a certain fluidity and an unavoidable tentativeness
to the boundaries and definitions used in this branch of science
just as in any other department of knowledge.

II. Subdivisions

The main divisions of the field of parapsychology are derived
from the two broad types of observed phenomena with which it
deals: *extrasensory perception* and *psychokinesis*. These phenomena, like all psychical (psychological) occurrences, whether
spontaneous or experimental, consist either of reports of subjective experiences on the one hand or of observed physical effects
on the other. In the experiences of extrasensory perception which
make up the more familiar division of parapsychical phenomena,
knowledge is acquired in a special way—by a mode of perception
that is independent of the senses. In one of these cognitive experiences an individual may seem to be looking upon a distant
scene somewhat as though he were physically there. In such
cases there is usually no difficulty in observing that information
was received, although in other kinds of parapsychical experiences
the individual may have indirect evidence of knowledge without
conscious certainty of the fact or may be impelled to a certain
course of action without at the time being aware of the reason for
so doing.

This use of the terms "knowledge" and "experience" to cover a
wide range of responses to external events when there is no sensory basis is a concession to convenience; but from now on we can
be more precise. Since the knowledge conveyed in a parapsychical occurrence concerns events external to the subject, technically
the mental process is properly called a *perception*. Since the
senses are not involved (and, with no physical mediation from the

object to the percipient such as characterizes sensory perception, they could not be) these cognitive phenomena of parapsychology are called *extrasensory perception* or ESP.

The other main subdivision of the phenomena of parapsychology includes all those occurrences in which, again without physical intermediation, some personal influence produces a physical effect. Such direct mental operation on a material body or a physical energy system is called *psychokinesis or PK*. This is the same as the familiar popular concept of mind over matter.

These two main branches of parapsychology, the phenomena of ESP and PK, appear to parallel the system already familiar to general psychology, the sensorimotor relations between subject and object. In both sensory perception and ESP the subject responds to or shows some degree of knowledge of an external event. And on the side of the reaction of the subject to the object, both in the already familiar motor responses and in PK, the individual mentally exerts an effect upon some part of the physical environment. The one fundamental difference that is most obvious is that in his sensorimotor relations with the objective environment the subject relies upon energies that have been already identified and to a large extent understood by physicists.

In ESP and PK, then, the subject interacts with the objective environment in a way for which there is no physical explanation and no acceptable physical hypothesis. Rather, the evidence indictates that the psychophysical interoperations of ESP and PK involve a basis that is not as yet known or observed except through the aftereffects shown in the experiences and experiments with which parapsychology is concerned. Not only has no intermediating process or principle yet been discovered but, thus far in the functioning of either ESP or PK, no specialized organs of reception or motor function have been localized. Thus it may be said that between the ESP-PK system and the sensorimotor system there is a general parallel of mind-matter relation even while there is also what seems at this stage of scientific inquiry to be a very fundamental difference.

The relationship between ESP and PK is still only partially understood. The view that has gained widest acceptance is that the two operations involve essentially the same sort of psychophysical interaction. The end results of the two processes or functions—if they are really different—are, of course, manifestly distinct effects. In the one case the result is an experience related to an external situation; in the other, an observable physical effect. Whether the occurrence be a spontaneous one or the result of an experimental test, these differences are phenomenologically distinct enough to justify the use of the two subdivisions, extrasensory perception and psychokinesis. But as the reader becomes familiar with the nature of these capacities and their way of functioning he will find it easy and convenient to use a general term to designate the whole range of parapsychical phenomena, and for this the Greek letter *psi* has come into general use. This is a device of convenience and does not imply that it is *known* that there is only one basic underlying type of process.

ESP phenomena of three general types are commonly recognized. These distinctions, too, are only partial and tentative ones. In fact, these three general classifications of ESP effects are mere descriptive terms that were applied to the phenomena as they came to be identified in the early stages of the developing science. But while they are comparatively arbitrary classifications, they have been so widely used in the literature and practice of the research that they are not likely to be abandoned for some time.

The two most familiar subdivisions of ESP, telepathy and clairvoyance, were in general use long before the term "extrasensory perception" itself was accepted. *Telepathy,* originally defined as the transfer of thought from one mind to another without the intermediation of the senses, is the effect which was most emphasized in the early period of psi investigation and it has, therefore, received the widest popular attention. In recent decades, however, the experimental work in parapsychology has been preponderantly concerned with clairvoyance. *Clairvoyance* is defined as the extrasensory perception of objects or objective events, as distinguished from the mental states or thoughts of another person. As the science of parapsychology has advanced, the basic similarity of the processes of telepathy and clairvoyance has become more and more apparent. It now seems doubtful whether they are two different processes after all. At any rate, it would be difficult to offer any specific fundamental difference between the two types of manifestation of ESP except, of course, in the targets perceived—the one subjective and the other objective.

The third category under ESP is generally called *precognition*. This is simply the perception of a future event by means of ESP. To qualify as a genuine instance of precognition an experience must refer to a coming event to an extent that is more than merely accidental; it must identify a future happening that could not have been inferred as about to occur; and, finally, it must refer to an event that could not have been brought about as a consequence of the prediction.

For the present stage of parapsychology these four general subdivisions—extrasensory perception and psychokinesis, with the former further subdivided into telepathy, clairvoyance, and pre-cognition—serve well enough for the necessary exchange of ideas and the discussion of results. As will be seen in the later chapters these subdivisions which have been reflected in the spontaneous psi experiences from which the branch of science arose have been confirmed by the experimental studies that have resulted. Thus far no other clear-cut subdivision has been found necessary or justifiable; and the impression is given that these four types of parapsychical phenomena are the result of a single underlying psi function. In any case, a fundamental relation between the subject and the object that is in some degree nonphysical has been established.

III. Relations to Other Areas

The present distinction between parapsychology and general psychology is fairly obviously a temporary one. Parapsychical phenomena are distinguishable from the other phenomena of psychology merely by the fact that they can be *shown* to be non-physical in character. With regard to the rest of the more purely psychological processes there is no way of telling whether non-physical operations play any part. Some theorists in psychology have taken the position that all mental life is essentially non-physical; but this interpretation was made on philosophical grounds. What science itself will discover about the rest of the domain of psychology we need not try to predict.

The relation of psi to the world of physics and physiology is
more clear-cut than its relation to general psychology. Here there
are demonstrable criteria of differentiation. The fact that psi
functions so far show no limiting influence of space and time
reveals a distinction that is perhaps the most fundamental yet
encountered in the entire universe of knowledge. The evidence is
now conclusive enough in parapsychology to leave no doubt that,
so far as present concepts go, we are dealing with nonphysical
principles and processes. Even so, the distinction is only relatively thoroughgoing. The psi function is in all instances the
result of an interaction between an organism and its environment;
and in the latter a physical system is always in some way involved.
Even in telepathy, with a supposedly "mind-to-mind" transfer,
there has in all verified instances been a physical brain coordinated
with the sender's thought. Science has not yet discovered enough
about the relation of mind and brain to say how far the distinction
can be carried between these two systems and whether the apparent dualism is anything more than a relative distinction. The
occurrence of interaction between psychical and physical systems
implies to the logical mind a basic unity suggesting that the
phenomena of parapsychology and physics are both of the same
all-embracing universe. If so then a larger scope of reality is still
to be disclosed than has been as yet revealed. Physics, then, is
not unrelated to psi and its operation. We can say, rather, only
that psi is not describable in terms of physical processes.

The extent to which psi is found to be a generalized capacity
among living behaving organisms will determine what and how
significant its place should be in the larger field of biology. For
the present this is a question under active research.

Since psi is definitely a *human* capacity, at least, and since the
nature of personality is fundamentally important to a wide range
of human relations, a broad area of significant possibilities should
be listed here if completeness in this outline of relations were to
be required. It is particularly important to consider what difference the establishment of psi as a human characteristic will make
to the larger disciplines concerned with human society. The discovery in man of properties not attributable to physical law gives
to the theory and philosophy of human relations a distinctly anti-

materialistic quality that is revolutionary and far-reaching. For religion it gives a scientific rebuttal to materialism; for ethics and mental hygiene it removes the road-block of mechanism; and for medicine, psychotherapy, and education it provides a scientific status for the common-sense concept that there is something in the subjective life of man that has distinctive principles of its own. It is safe to say that when the recognition of psi as a nonphysical component of human personality has occurred, there will hardly be any area of human relations untouched by the significance of this generalization.

IV. Clarification of Terms and Concepts

The term *parapsychology* was adapted from the German word, *Parapsychologie,* the most widely used of the European terms which identify the field. It means the same as the older English expression, *psychical research,* and the French, *métapsychique.* *Psychical* is an ambiguous word, being used in general psychology to mean "mental." The popular use of the word *psychic,* while convenient and well-entrenched, has the same ambiguity.

The prefix *para* added to psychology (and psychical) serves well enough the purpose of marking off a section of the general field of psychology for such time as the distinction is needed. But it is not to be applied loosely as a generally valid prefix for other similar uses in the field. For example, the terms *paraphysical, paraphysiological, paranormal,* and the like, are not sufficiently clear-cut in their meaning to justify their use. *Paranormal* has a certain amount of current usage as an equivalent of parapsychical, but like its predecessors, *supernormal* and *supernatural,* it seems to carry the quite erroneous (and unintended) implication that psi phenomena are not a normal part of nature. *Normal* is itself a word of too many proper as well as improper meanings to be used reliably in terminology and definition.

The term *extrasensory perception* which came to general use in 1934 has proved to be more useful than its alternatives, such as *super-sensory perception, ultra-perceptive faculty, paranormal cognition, metagnomy,* etc. It has probably survived because it has fitted the need for a descriptive expression that implies no untested theory as to its nature.

The word *telepathy* came into use around the beginning of the century to describe what had been called thought-transference (mental telegraphy, etc.). It is redundant to use the modifying adjective *mental* to describe telepathy.

Clairvoyance is perhaps the oldest term in general use in parapsychology and it has outlasted a number of expressions that were introduced to describe the extrasensory perception of objec‑ tive events, of which the following are the most common: *lucidity, telesthesia, cryptesthesia.* Efforts to introduce related terms such as *clairaudience* and *clairsentience* have failed because the term *clairvoyance* is not limited to its etymological derivation, "clear-seeing." *Psychometry* has had a wide usage in parapsychology for what may more appropriately be referred to as *token-object tests* of ESP (i.e., identification of people and events associated with an object by means of ESP). The term psychometry has an established use in general psychology in its proper sense of mental measurement, and it should not be abused in any parapsychological application.

The introduction of *precognition* to identify the ESP of future events logically suggested the term *retrocognition* for the ESP of past occurrences. However, there is no adequately verified psi phenomenon to which *retrocognition* itself may be applied.

At the time of the introduction of *psychokinesis* there was a choice between it and the term *telekinesis,* mainly associated with physical manifestations connected with the claim of medium-ship. *Telekinesis* means "action at a distance," and psychokinesis, "the direct action of mind upon matter." The use of the latter term was preferred as more accurate and as more clearly having no limiting connotation of discarnate agency.

A number of efforts have already been made to provide a systematic general nomenclature for parapsychology. They have, however, all been premature and no such attempt has at best contributed more than perhaps a single accepted term or two to general usage in the field. Obviously the effective and accepted application of a systematized terminology will call for a well-organized rationale of the phenomena to be dealt with. But parapsychology has only recently reached the status of organization presented here. It will require a period of time for a sufficient familiarization with this pattern of findings to occur before the field will need a more systematic set of descriptive terms.

Parapsychology needs also to be distinguished from popular concepts connected with certain areas of practice or belief which are sometimes confused or associated with it. *Occultism* is one of these. This term designating the study of hidden arts or principles does not apply to the scientific type of approach that characterizes parapsychology. *Spiritualism* is another term that has been widely associated with parapsychology. Spiritualism, however, is a religion, having for its central emphasis belief in the existence of a world of discarnate personalities supposedly able to communicate with the living, mainly through mediumship. They are also believed capable of manifestations such as hauntings and poltergeist phenomena (a sort of rough-housing attributed to noisy spirits). As with all religious systems of belief, there are certain doctrines in spiritualism based upon the assumption of capacities that have not been verified by scientific method in parapsychology. The relationship of parapsychology to areas possibly involving its principles is, in general, something like that of a pure to an applied science area. There is the important difference, however, that in no instance in parapsychology as yet has such application grown out of preceding laboratory discovery.

Certain of the terms more commonly associated with spiritualism have come into widespread popular usage; for example, the terms *medium* and *mediumship*. Strictly speaking, the term *medium* implies a theory of spirit survival and of communication of discarnate personalities with the living through the intermediation of persons known as mediums. This is a doctrine in the Spiritualist faith and is not a scientifically established fact in parapsychology. It is, however, correct to say that the investigation of the hypothesis of spirit survival and communication would be a parapsychological one (see Chapter 6).

The distinction between parapsychology and *psychopathology* ought to be made clear, since textbooks on abnormal psychology have often included them both without adequate distinction. There is no implication of pathology in anything associated with parapsychology; and, on its part, psychopathology has traced none of its causal factors to the domain of parapsychology (see Chapter 6).

Hypnosis or hypnotism was for a long period of its history associated with psi phenomena, especially in its aspect of "somnambulism"; but as the studies of both hypnotism and parapsychology have advanced, the independence of the two classes of phenomena has become amply clear. Similarly, the vaguely defined state known as (self-induced) *trance* has passed through a similar evolution; as have also the various motor automatisms (unconscious muscular movements) such as dowsing, automatic writing, and the use of the ouija board. Gradually, through advancing understanding, the phenomena of parapsychology have emerged as distinct from these earlier associations and are now describable and demonstrable in their own characteristic properties.

Additional Reading

EDITORIAL: A proposed basis for choosing terms in parapsychology. *J. Parapsychol.,* 9:147–149, 1945.

EDITORIAL: Pattern of history in parapsychology. *J. Parapsychol.,* 17:247–258, 1953.

JAMES, WM.: The confidences of a "psychical researcher." *American Magazine,* pp. 580–589, Oct., 1909.

LODGE, O.: The university aspect of psychical research, in *The Case For and Against Psychical Belief.* Worcester, Mass., Clark Univ. Press, 1927, pp. 3–14.

McDOUGALL, WM.: Psychical research as a university study, in *The Case for and Against Psychical Belief.* Worcester, Mass., Clark Univ. Press, 1927, pp. 149–162.

McDOUGALL, WM.: Editorial introduction. *J. Parapsychol.,* 1:1–9, 1937.

MURPHY, G.: *Challenge of Psychical Research.* New York, Harper, 1961, pp. 1-6; 274-291.

MURPHY, G.: Parapsychology, in *Encyclopedia of Psychology.* New York, Philosophical Library, 1946, pp. 417–436.

MURPHY, G.: The place of parapsychology among the sciences. *J. Parapsychol.,* 13:62–71, 1949.

MYERS, F. W. H.: *Human Personality and its Survival of Bodily Death.* New York, Longmans, 1954.

RHINE, J. B.: *Extrasensory Perception.* Boston, Bruce Humphries, 1934, pp. 5—14. Paperback Edition, 1962.

RHINE, J. B.: Introduction to experimental parapsychology, in *Present-day Psychology.* New York, Philosophical Library, 1955, pp. 469–486.

RHINE, J. B.: Parapsychology, in *The New Outline of Modern Knowledge.* New York, Simon and Schuster, 1956, pp. 193–211.

RHINE, J. B.: *The Reach of the Mind.* New York, Wm. Sloane, 1947.

RHINE, J. B., et al.: *Extrasensory Perception After Sixty Years.* New York, Holt, 1940, pp. 3–21.

SIDGWICK, H.: Presidential address. *Proc. Soc. Psych. Res.,* 1:7–12, 1882.

THOULESS, R. H.: Thought transference and related phenomena, in *Proc. Roy. Institution of Great Britain,* 1950.

TYRRELL, G. N. M.: *Science and Psychical Phenomena.* New York, Harper, 1938.

Chapter 2

Objective Research Methods

I. Introduction

A FIELD of science should properly be judged on the basis of its methods of investigation. In parapsychology, however, as in any branch of psychology where there are subjective or mental factors and conditions to be dealt with, a consideration of the *objective* methods alone is not enough. As a matter of fact, there is even a question as to whether they come first in importance. But for the purpose of this book it will be advantageous to present the objective methods first and deal with the important consideration of psychological methods and conditions of experimentation later (Chapter 7). The reasoning is that an appreciation of the sound status of the facts of parapsychology should come first, and for that the objective methods are clearly of prior importance. After this first step is taken, then the shift of interest to other problems makes the psychological conditions the more important in their turn.

By objective methods we do not mean only the specific testing techniques by means of which the investigations are made. The standardized test procedures generally used in the study of psi phenomena are, of course, an essential part of the methods; the main types of procedure are described in Chapter 8. Likewise, the mathematical techniques that play an important part in measuring the degree to which the experimental results exceed the level expected from pure chance are an essential part of the objective methods; they are given in Chapter 9. These descriptions of the more specialized techniques, while they are essential to research and clinical use, are not necessary here for an appreciation of the general way in which psi has been investigated.

17

LIBRARY ST. MARY'S COLLEGE

Thus, as we have just indicated, three major sections of what might be broadly considered as methods in parapsychology are considered in another section of the volume. This leaves for the present chapter the general program of how, in concretely describable fashion, research in parapsychology is done; how its questions arise; how, and how reliably, they are answered.

It should be said at the outset that because of the challenge of the findings of parapsychology, the research workers have a greater consciousness of method and of rigorous control than is found in other branches of science. The radical nature of the results have also made it necessary to develop a wider range of safeguards against error than in any other field. This is, however, altogether proper when revolutionary conclusions are drawn. Within reasonable limits such added precautions must be taken.

A few people, it is true, have questioned whether it is possible for science to deal effectively and exhaustively with such non-physical functions as are investigated in parapsychology. The very strangeness and elusiveness of some of the human experiences dealt with in this field tend to raise questions concerning the full adequacy of such methods. But we need only remember that physics itself, as well as other curricular branches of knowledge, have long been working at least partly with extrasensory phenomena—operations and effects that are clearly beyond the range of the sense organs. They are, of course, not connected with personality or mental life and, therefore, are not parapsychical; but, like psi capacities, they can be measured only by their indirect effects. Most of the researches in general psychology, too, depend upon this indirect approach. The general principle followed is that anything in the universe man will ever know about creates effects; and through these effects it can be indirectly studied, even if the process itself is beyond the range of the senses and even beyond reach of the instruments that so greatly extend the range of the senses.

In theory, at least, it should be possible for science to investigate any real phenomenon, any true operation in the universe; and we can advance as far as we have the patience and ingenuity to go toward satisfying ourselves of its genuine occurrence. Moreover, if the first inquirers are able to describe their methods clearly as they proceed, others, too, if they are prepared, can then follow the trail, confirm its existence, and improve or extend it still further.

II. The Two Stages of Scientific Method

Science has two fairly obvious general functions. One of these is its role of *exploration* or discovery, the turning up of new phenomena or ideas; the other is the task of *verification* or the making sure whether a claimed discovery or suggested hypothesis is valid. Both are essential, and one is as important as the other. Moreover, it is extremely important for worker and student alike to keep both of these two types of scientific inquiry in mind, and above all to keep each with its proper requirements in its proper place. This is not always done in actual practice. Many students of science who are mainly concerned with but one of these two stages of scientific inquiry tend to forget that there *is* another too. Some, of course, are largely unaware of methods as such; they are casually following a heritage of custom established by habit and routine.

The chief characteristic of the exploratory stage of scientific inquiry is that in it the explorer is permitted to range widely, venture freely, and look into everything that might be important to his interest without being burdened with too much precautionary concern. It is a more venturesome, a more extravagant phase of investigation. It is always a first stage, of course, but only because of the natural order of investigation. While it is obvious that without this exploratory stage there would be little or nothing for science to verify or establish, it is equally true that with it alone no results would ever be firmly established.

On the other hand, the second or conclusive stage of research has very different characteristics. Its emphasis is mainly on reliability. The starting point is a claim or hypothesis to be put to crucial test and the first step is the drawing up of an experimental plan carefully designed to take all the alternatives into account. The testing itself must be done with constant vigilance to see that the requirements laid down in the plan are fully met. Equally important, perhaps, are the soundness of logic used in interpreting the results and the careful suspension of judgment regarding conclusions until the accepted standards of science are met—standards of adequate experimental control, of extrachance(statistical) significance, and of independent confirmation by other investigators.

The most common violation of good method, at least in parapsychology, lies in the much too ready confusion of these two phases of science—exploration and verification. For example, an overanxious inquirer may (like a scout setting out with heavy battle equipment) attempt to carry the complex controls of verification along with him when he is setting forth on purely exploratory activities. Equally common is the reverse emphasis in which a research worker jumps to premature and unwarranted conclusions on the strength of what are no more than exploratory findings. He does not feel the need of waiting for the slow, firm test of crucial investigation. There are many variations of these familiar violations of good procedure; they are not, of course, limited to parapsychology. As we have already said, however, there has been good reason for workers in this field to become especially conscious of methods and standards.

III. Exploratory Methods in Parapsychology

The ways of exploratory inquiry in parapsychology are substantially the same as those used in other comparable fields. One of them is the elementary method of studying reports of exceptional spontaneous occurrences and generalizing from such a study to an hypothesis that can be put to test or a claim that can be examined by means of other methods. This is the *case-study method*. A second method of exploration, identified as the *preliminary individual test*, is adapted to the introductory study of special persons such as, for example, those whose behavior or experience suggests unusual psi powers. The third way of screening projects for more conclusive investigation by trying them out on a small scale in a preliminary way is called the *pilot test method*. Fourth, much valuable exploratory work is done by going over the data of earlier experiments. Re-examined with fresh problems in mind, these records often contribute new insights not glimpsed during the original investigation. This is the *method of re-examination*.

In all of these four methods (the principal ones that have been followed) the purpose is to make a discovery, at least a tentative one; this becomes a new hypothesis for further investigation. Thus the end point of an exploratory investigation is a new and important question, one that deserves for its reliable answering the more refined treatment of a crucial test. A brief discussion of each of these methods will give a better idea of how most of the research in parapsychology has actually been done. As in any field of science, more time and effort are generally needed on the exploratory stage of a problem than for the conclusive stage of research.

A. Case-Study Method

Originally, parapsychology as a science began with reports of spontaneous personal experiences of unexplainable nature. In the early studies emphasis was placed upon the need to authenticate such cases as allowed careful checking on the reliability of reporting. It became evident, however, that even elaborate effort in substantiating them did not furnish sufficiently unquestionable evidence to warrant a conclusion. The hypothesis was too revolutionary. Experimental methods had to be introduced for that purpose. The case study is by its nature primarily an exploratory method; it would be difficult if not impossible to convert it into a crucial method of verification.

At the present stage of parapsychology, the case method provides a very important source of suggestions as to the nature and properties of psi as it functions spontaneously. The research worker can, with advantage (beginning either with an appropriate case collection already available or by making one of his own) ask his questions of Nature as represented in these experiences. If it be a specific question as to how psi operates spontaneously, and if the collection be suitable and the question answerable, he should be able to get a tentative answer. This trial-answer or hypothesis may be impressively evident or it may be but slightly indicated. No matter how strong the appearance of support, however, the tentative new idea is still based on the reports of human experiences which cannot be sufficiently validated to permit a scientific conclusion to be reached.

But there is some preliminary testing of an idea that can profitably be done within the case method itself. A question or
hypothesis raised from one collection of cases can be checked
against another or even more than one. A confirmation from a
second large collection would considerably strengthen the status
of the hypothesis, though it would definitely still not provide conclusive verification. To mention only one possibility of weakness,
the two collections might have a common defect, perhaps one in-
herent in the cultural influence affecting them both or in the
method by which the two collections had been assembled. But
such support as a second collection might give would go far to
warrant the large effort which experimental verification calls
for. In this way could be worked up the pressure of confidence
and challenge needed before the much greater outlay of research
time and other resources demanded by the conclusive test would
be undertaken. It is not, in fact, justifiable to undertake the
more crucial stage of testing until the exploratory build-up has at
least answered the principal objections that may be raised and
has developed a reasonably probable case. This much can be
done by the case method when it is used to best effect.

Collections of psi cases will, of course, vary according to col-
lectors and also according to the instructions issued regarding the
types of cases desired. It is best to make a new collection and to
secure broad coverage of types; in older collections the persons
reporting the cases may have been given too selective instructions. In the same way it would be wise not to require any
specific standard of reporting or authentication since thereby
many cases for which there could be no corroborative support
possible would be excluded. Since the purpose is to discover
Nature's own way of demonstrating such phenomena, it would
be defeating the purpose of exploration to rule out at the collection point, just because they seemed less impressive from the point
of view of evidentiality, any types of cases that could have bearing
on research problems. In recognizing the tentative status of the
case study results, the explorer can be relieved of misplaced
anxiety over the reliability of a report.

Case study methods involve much that need not be considered
here at length. They depend, of course, on the logical judgment

exercised in making analyses. If a question is asked of a case collection, it needs to be clarified and the possible answers stated clearly enough for definite understanding by others. The standards of analysis need to be defined so plainly that another worker can follow and, if desired, re-analyze the same material. Results must, of course, be stated when appropriate in quantitative form as percentages or ratios and, when justified, the distributions may be tested for extrachance significance by a chi square method (see Chapter 9).

The cases referred to thus far were those of the spontaneous type occurring to the individual, but in a more general way the same method of exploration applies to all nonexperimental items of observation that can be grouped or collected for general comparison and analysis. Instances of observation among professional workers in related fields such as anthropology, psychiatry, and religion and among such practices as dowsing and mediumship should be studied in their preliminary stages by essentially similar exploratory methods.

B. Individual Screening Method

Probably the exploratory practices in widest use are those of examining and screening individual subjects, either for participation in more conclusive experimental work or for a more elaborate exploratory program. Most commonly in such preliminary tests the investigator is dealing with a person who believes on some basis or other that he is gifted with psi capacity and wishes to know the extent of his ability. The contact between him and the experimenter may have arisen as a result of the individual's own curiosity over his spontaneous experiences or he may have been referred to the research worker by a teacher, psychiatrist, or minister. In any case, a widely adaptable preliminary test method is needed for this purpose, one that will lend itself to a variety of conditions while still affording a reasonably accurate estimate of the ability concerned.

It has been greatly advantageous, indeed, to have certain *standard* methods of testing available, methods with an already existing frame of reference into which results may be placed for comparative judgment. The widespread use of the standard ESP card test, with a five-symbol pack of 25 cards developed at the Duke University Parapsychology Laboratory, makes it more efficient to follow an adaptation of this method; a wide basis of comparison is automatically provided. The fact that there are five possible choices makes 20 per cent success the level of scoring to be expected from pure chance. If for any reason the subject to be tested has an expressed preference, the five symbols of the standard deck (star, circle, square, cross, waves) can be replaced by a set of five colors, five animal pictures, or any other suitable set of items. In fact, there are advantages in these local adaptations.

But there again availability has the advantage; and the standard deck of ESP cards mentioned above has not only been the most widely used in the ESP researches of the last 25 years, but it is at present the most conveniently available.*

Above all, however, the method to be used needs to suit the subject's interest and preparation. If, for example, he shows any hesitation to use a test that makes possible definite scoring (and mathematical evaluation), a preliminary test could use other target material (e.g., pictures cut from magazines). It is wise to start with whatever the subject believes is the best for him. The change to other and better conditions can be made later, once success in scoring has been demonstrated and the subject's confidence established. Should a subject fail in preliminary tests, it would be much better for him to do so on tests which he has been fully ready to accept and approve. If he does fail persistently from the start and no variation of conditions over a number of sessions can induce success, there is nothing to do but discontinue; only if, and as long as, he is giving a moderate show of successful scoring is it profitable to try to improve and advance the test conditions.

Once, however, a subject shows special ability under free, informal conditions, the next step is to introduce safeguards. This should, for psychological reasons, always be done with a subject's full approval and cooperation. With continual improvement of

---

* To keep the copyrighted standard cards available, authority to distribute them is restricted in the U.S.A. to Haines House of Cards, Norwood, Ohio, and its distributing agencies.

conditions the point will be reached at which the experimental controls will be sufficiently rigorous to meet the full requirements of verification. When that point is reached, the proper procedure is to go right into it as if no real distinction were involved. The line between advanced exploration and initial verification is, in any case, an arbitrary one. The subject himself is usually the better for not having the strain of being told he is facing a crucial test. In general, any neglect of the delicate psychological conditions that psi subjects require for effective demonstration is wasteful. We assume, however, that Chapter 7 on the psychological conditions for psi tests will be taken into account with this one.

It is essential, too, that the experimenter have some knowledge of what to expect from a subject—that is, how to judge the rate of scoring. He needs to know as the tests progress how well his subject is doing if only to know when to advance or to change over to the next stage. While it is important to allow the new subject to begin with any preferred condition he may have in mind and to allow an amply successful demonstration on this level before adding precautions, if a subject has no set ideas and no predilections as to methods it is of advantage to start with conditions that rule out as many of the conceivable errors as possible. With that in mind, we recommend a clairvoyance test rather than one for GESP or general extrasensory perception. A GESP test makes no attempt to distinguish between telepathy and clairvoyance (for example, the sender looks at the target card during the trial). A clairvoyance test requires only one subject, instead of the two needed wherever telepathy may also be involved. It also eliminates for the experimenter any concern over possible sensory communication between sender and receiver. Even if the subject prefers GESP, he may be persuaded or challenged to try clairvoyance after some initial success with the other method. If not, and the GESP test has to be used to start with, it is important, even on the exploratory level, to advance the test procedure so that two rooms are used, with the sender in one and the receiver in the other, and with the connecting door closed.

But with clairvoyance test methods the advance to adequate precautions can be more rapid and the evidential value of the results accordingly greater. If the subject is not hesitant, the test can begin with the cards screened entirely from all sensory contact, even in the very first test. Then, with the experimenter keeping records of all scores for a full appraisal and with a method of double witnessing (by subject and experimenter) of the card recording and scoring, the method should be sufficiently safe for this preliminary order of testing. The basic requirements for safeguarding the procedure and for evaluating the results will be found in Chapters 8 and 9.

It should be possible to develop testing devices that would be so adaptable to diverse situations and individual needs that (when they are properly used) the most free and informal ESP test would be fully safeguarded. Progress toward this ideal is highly desirable especially since there are many clinical, educational, and other practical adaptations of the ESP test that are awaiting such a development. But it is no less necessary here than elsewhere to emphasize again that the requisite psychological conditions discussed in Chapter 7 would also have to be met or the test could not be considered in any real sense an ESP test at all.

C. Pilot-Study Method

The third exploratory procedure in parapsychology makes use of a small trial research preliminary to a larger, more thorough one. It already has had a fair amount of use and it has been of great value to the field. It is especially needed to offset the tendency of overenthusiastic experimenters to plunge into elaborately designed projects right from the start. Some investigators who have been successful in other stages of scientific work assume, unjustifiably, that they will naturally succeed, too, in conducting psi experiments in what they assume to be a comparably proper and effective manner. They reason that since others have succeeded they should expect to do so, and that since they have done competent research in other areas they should be expected to get results in parapsychology as well. But this is to overlook the many uncontrolled variables that are usually present in the psychological experiment and are especially likely to cause trouble in investigations with so elusive a capacity as psi.

It is in just such a case that a small pilot experiment can serve a very useful purpose—in fact, a number of purposes. The experimenter can first of all satisfy himself that he has what is required as an experimenter to bring out psi capacity in the subjects with whom he expects to work. He can at the same time assemble a selected team of subjects and settle many other initial questions involving experimental conditions. If a preliminary experiment is clear-cut and indicative he then will know what to do on the main project. If the pilot study is discouraging, more preparation or modification of the design is in order and perhaps further preliminary researches. It is, of course, important to keep in mind that the pilot experiment is definitely exploratory and that, whatever its results, they are to be considered apart from the major project which it serves to introduce.

One of the main values of the pilot study method in parapsychology springs from the need in this new branch to fend off wild theorists who approach the field with an unduly speculative bent. These rationalists would start off on an ambitious program to demonstrate their theories. They are usually difficult to persuade to try out first, on a preliminary scale, the wholly unsupported expectations they have built up. There is little to be gained from these impulsive attempts to launch a full-scale conclusive research project at their early stage of investigation. The pilot test stands ready to help the researcher, whether beginner or professional, to fit his experiments more effectively to his project.

D. The Re-examination Method

Fourth in the types of exploratory methods in general use in parapsychology is that in which old data are re-examined for other purposes than the original investigators had in mind. After an experimental series has been evaluated and reported for what it was intended to do, the author or another worker has in many instances had reason to re-examine the data in search of the answer to a different question from the original one. Many of the leading developments of the last quarter century in parapsychology owe their origin or support to this device of incidental exploring.

The method is more than merely a search among old records for overlooked significance. It follows a more or less systematic course, in broad outline much like that of the case-study method. The researcher in need of an answer to a question turns toward whatever relevant available data he can find. He might be, let us say, asking whether the scoring rate in PK tests falls off in the course of a run (or column), as it does in ESP. Why should he trouble to carry out a new experiment to explore this possibility when there are files of old data to examine? Thus the old material, when it could answer the question, has often acquired a later value which its original producer never anticipated.

It is true the first discovery in such a case would have only the tentative value of any exploratory finding. Almost immediately, however, the research worker may "predict" (that is, reasonably infer) that a similar result would be found in a comparable batch of old data still unexamined; and if this new program is well planned and properly handled, the magic line of verification itself can be crossed in the very next stride. This possibility of a quick changeover to a method of crucial test is one of the greatest values of this method. As we stated, there has been a very productive reclamation program in parapsychology. If we keep in mind that the takeoff by this reclamation method is always an exploratory research, we shall not make undue claims for its results until further (predicted) reclamation verifies the first result.

E. Methods for Clinical and Other Practical Uses

A broad category of methods remains that, while not exploratory in the sense that we have been using the term, is comparable in many respects. These might be called clinical or practical methods; that is, ways of adapting psi tests to particular situations involving professional service in other areas than parapsychological research. Suppose, for example, that a clinical psychologist or psychiatrist needs to test a patient's belief that he is especially endowed with a psi capacity. This somewhat resembles the situation in which the *Individual Screening Method* described above is used preparatory to a more controlled research. The purpose, however, may be entirely subordinate to some such objective as diagnosis or treatment, and the standards required should be those which the professional practitioner will need to have for his purposes.

For such needs, whether they arise in connection with patients or in anthropological field studies, or in educational projects involving special children, or in any other of the many possible situations in which the question of unusual mental powers may arise, the general recommendation might be much the same. In a word, the adaptation of the standard testing techniques can, until specialized modifications have been developed for a given clinical purpose, be managed in much the same way as exploratory testing of other individual subjects. The same relative care will be needed as in all psi testing to see that psychological conditions are properly met and to avoid imposing upon the subject to be tested a too artificial method or one he does not adequately understand or fully accept. Indeed, the rule should be rigidly imposed on the would-be experimenter to meet the subject's requirements as fully and carefully as if they were actually objective in character.

Standards of the clinical or practical tests may be laid down by the professional worker himself according to the needs of his situation. At one extreme they could be as high as those used in crucial tests. But for general use at the bedside, in school, or in field situations a somewhat rough and ready test will be found more suitable and all the precautions not specifically needed may be dropped. Counterhypotheses to psi that have never had any real support in fact (as, for example, involuntary whispering on the part of the agent in a test involving telepathy), and which have been given an exaggerated importance only because of the controversy over ESP, can profitably be forgotten in practical testing. This and the special precautions against possible errors in recording may safely be left to the more controlled researches in parapsychology proper. Those who wish to apply the methods to adjacent problem areas will in any case naturally make such modifications of method as they themselves feel are warranted by the conditions and demands of their purpose. For this purpose wide ranging clinical adaptations of testing techniques are necessary and entirely in order.

The four main exploratory methods just described were not designed by a logician; they just grew into usage and survived because they proved successful. There are certain inconsistencies and overlappings that could bother the meticulous thinker a little. For example, the concept of the *Pilot-Study Method* could be stretched in principle to include the *Individual Screening Method*. Also, the *Re-examination Method* can be so quickly converted to a fully verifying procedure that to single out the first stage as exploratory and then call the second verification (even though it may be a mere duplication) may seem a bit arbitrary. It is better, however, for the present to take these introductory fact-finding procedures as they are, since they are working successfully, and allow refinements of consistency and classification to develop with continued use and free discussion. There is certainly no crucial need for logical consistency since the methods are productive. Bringing them into explicit focus as we have done may, we trust, help both toward further clarification as well as more extensive use.

No absolute distinction marks the transition from exploratory research to the second stage of method to which we now turn, that of verification or establishment. Rather, the transition is first of all a change of emphasis in the objective or purpose of the research worker. He need not always change his actual test procedure; though he probably will. So great, however, is the consequence of the altered goal of the new stage that a very different tempo and tone of research develops. The stress shifts completely from venturesome search to cautious assaying, each in its turn playing an essential part.

IV. *Methods of Verification*

The scientific establishment of any fact is admittedly a relative matter. One's acceptance of a given finding or result often depends, for example, upon his personal attitude or philosophy. Whether one is conducting the research himself or only appraising a published report of it, he may reach a decision regarding the conclusiveness of the result without realizing the degree to which his mind was made up in advance. Accordingly, the candid explorer would do well to bring into conscious perspective at the beginning any assumptions or prejudgments of the problem he can discover in his approach. Otherwise, he might be undertaking the investigation with an attitude that would require for his acceptance that it turn out in a definite, limited way; and if it did not, he would be prone to reject the results on some ground or other. There is even danger in a psychological experiment that such an attitude might so influence investigation that accuracy would be affected. In general, it is exceedingly questionable whether any experiment is worth doing *until* the investigator himself is psychologically and philosophically prepared to take the consequences seriously, whatever they may be.

We shall, therefore, assume that for a conclusive experiment we have an experimenter prepared to accept the results in an objective manner. What kind of methods, then, are needed for the crucial task of verifying an hypothesis in parapsychology?

A. Statistical Evaluation

First, there is the requirement of sound measurement. In parapsychology this has to do with the estimation of significance with respect to chance. So long as psi capacity is in need of investigation, there will always have to be provision to deal with chance as a possible explanation of results. In a word, statistics is needed in any branch of science for the investigation of functions not yet fully understood and controllable at will. Accordingly, when designing the scope and size of the experiment, it is necessary to take thought and record in advance just what means will be used to evaluate the results. For most problems of parapsychology, fortunately, standard methods of applied statistics serve very well and there is little need for the novel and distinctive in this aspect of the field. The use of the principal methods has been expressly approved by both individual and group authority in statistics. These main techniques are described in Chapter 9 (as well as in the textbooks on statistics listed there).

The test procedures that have been most widely used have been chosen and developed partly with a view to making evaluation comparatively easy. For the ESP researches the techniques involving testing by means of cards have been most commonly relied on, and the use of dice in the PK research has so far dominated that branch of the inquiry. In the ESP investigations the requirement that there be a reasonable approximation to a random series of targets (card order) has been sufficiently well met to serve the needs of statistical theory by shuffling the cards and following with a thumbnail cut. But the card order may, for special purposes, be made up also on the basis of tables of random numbers.

In the measurement of the significance of rate of success in the tests, it has for the most part been adequate to use the oldest known procedure in parapsychological statistics as a yardstick. This method takes account of the total number of successes made in a given number of trials. It accurately estimates the number of hits to be expected on the theory of chance and finds the deviation of the hit total from this mean chance expectation. This deviation is then measured by means of (divided by) the standard deviation (SD); the quotient is the critical ratio (CR), a value which may be converted by means of the standard normal probability integral table to an equivalent probability. Thus an estimate is made of the likelihood that results as different from chance expectancy as those in question would occur in a pure chance series. This is the measure by which the investigator knows whether or not his results are acceptably significant; that is, may reasonably be classed as nonrandom events.

The ease with which the theoretical standard deviation is derived and the wide applicability of the method to the whole area of research in parapsychology for which standard methods of testing have been devised have done much to organize the field and to unify research activity within it. Results of the different researches can now be properly compared, combined, and, in general, treated in a systematic manner.

B. Experimental Precautions

The *second* basic requirement of a definitive research in parapsychology brings us to the aspect of experimental safeguards, and to the most important of these, the insurance that, in a crucial ESP test, there be absolutely no possibility of sensory communication. If a test is to be at all crucial, there is no excuse for using conditions that leave the question of sensory cues as one to be answered by judgment or interpretation.

The possibility of sensory cues can conveniently be eliminated in a card test of ESP, especially in a clairvoyance test; it is much easier in that type of ESP test than in one either of pure telepathy or one that allows for the possibility of telepathy (GESP). If there is no special reason for including telepathy, therefore, the test should by all means be carried out without a sender or agent present who is aware of the card order. Almost all of the difficulties that have arisen in controlling against sensory cues have come up in tests of GESP. It is obviously a simple matter in a clairvoyance test to screen a pack of cards entirely from a subject's view, and such screening is necessary if a test is to be conclusive. With an ordinary opaque screen large enough to rule out any possibility that the subject might see around its edges, the pack of cards can be conveniently handled by the experimenter under adequate conditions of control. Watchfulness against sensory observation of the target in reflecting surfaces or through crevices is unnecessary if, in addition, the experimenter "plays his cards close," that is, keeps the target card always in a guardedly safe location behind the screen and face down.

A number of modified clairvoyance testing techniques involve some elaboration of this simple screened card test. The cards may be enclosed in opaque envelopes or boxes that are then sealed, or there may be greater distance interposed between the subject and the cards by using different rooms, or even different buildings or geographic areas. Again, in addition to the calling techniques just described are those known as ESP matching techniques, tests in which an unknown card is matched against a set of "key" cards containing one of each type of symbol. The order of these latter may be either known or unknown by the subject. The various modifications are not different enough in principle to call for discussion. The main techniques themselves are given in Chapter 8.

If a research project involves telepathy, the requirement for a conclusive test calls for two rooms right from the start. Such separation will call for a method of communication between the two rooms. This should be a one-way method permitting only the receiving subject or percipient to signal the agent when he is ready for the next trial. All sensory communication from the agent would be suspect and it is necessary to go to considerable length *to rule out the possibility* of communication, deliberate or unconscious, on the part of an agent in an adjoining room. If the distance can be considerably increased, it would be an added safeguard; if two people well known to each other are acting as sender and receiver, steps should be taken to eliminate the possibility of the use of concealed devices of modern radio communication. It is always advisable, too, in attempting a conclusive test of GESP to have the order of the cards recorded before the pack is turned over to the agent, and to require that the percipient indicate or record his responses in silence, allowing no possibility that the agent could, in hearing that the percipient's call scored a miss, shift the order of cards in such a way as to make the trial a hit.

It is a particular advantage of the standard precognition test that all problems relating to the danger of sensory cues are automatically eliminated. This advantage has even tempted some experimenters to use the method in an exploratory way, since all that is needed is to hand out a record sheet and ask the would-be subject to fill in the column with what he anticipates will be entered at the checking stage in the card column opposite. There is, of course, a question whether many subjects are psychologically prepared to undertake a test in precognition at so early a stage of acquaintance with psi testing.

In the standard tests of psychokinesis there is, likewise, no problem of sensory cues; but there is a somewhat comparable one in the need to eliminate the possibility of error due to physical imperfections in the dice or in the use of skilled methods of handling or releasing them so as to influence their fall. These problems have long since been adequately solved in a number of different ways. Any inequalities in the dice are, for example, adequately compensated for by the use of all the different faces of the die to an equal extent as the target objective. It has also been found possible in a variety of ways to avoid the risk that the subject may use trick throws to influence the fall of the dice in PK tests. One way is to require the use of a dice cup with a sufficiently roughened interior and also deep enough to prevent the application of manual skill to the roll of the dice. It has, likewise, been found practical to release the dice by electric switch, allowing them to fall from a V-shaped container onto a prepared (walled and padded) table. Likewise, electrically driven, rotating cages have been used which allow the dice to roll from one end of a long cage to another, giving sufficient time for them to come to rest at the lower end and allow observation and recording. At this point a photographic record can be made as a part of the automatic operation of the apparatus.

C. Care in Recording

A *third* general requirement for a proper experimental verification in parapsychology concerns the making of adequate records of the results. All the data of an experiment must be recorded in such a way as to eliminate any possibility of error that could produce spurious results. For this purpose, the ideally careful experiment needs to be set up in such a way that the responsibility is shared between two persons qualified by training and selection to produce a faithful record, shared in such a way that no error made by either one could go undetected. This is referred to as the *two-experimenter plan* and its application to the various types of experiment might briefly be reviewed.

The two-experimenter plan in a simple clairvoyance experiment of the type already described may be managed in the following way: The record pad presented to the subject for the recording of his responses has a carbon inserted for duplication. The packs of cards to be used in a given run have been recorded in advance with one copy of the record in the possession of a second experimenter who may or may not be actually present in the experimental room at the time the test is being conducted. At the end of the run the subject is instructed to turn over his duplicate to the second experimenter or it may be inserted in the slit opening of a locked box prepared for the purpose (by the second experimenter). Then the first experimenter who is conducting the test can proceed to check the run with the subject participating, using the copies which they have of the card and call records. The second experimenter has his own copies of the records for safekeeping and for a wholly independent check. In this way, while errors could still be made, they could not be made in a way that would produce extra-chance effects without being caught.

There are, of course, many modifications of this two-experimenter method. One of these that is simpler in its routine and is widely used consists of loading a target sheet of symbols in a heavy, carefully-sealed manila envelope. The experimenter who does this keeps a carbon copy of the target sheet. The other experimenter asks the subject to register his responses on a record sheet (complete with carbon and a duplicate call sheet) attached to the outside of the envelope, responses intended to duplicate as far as possible the symbols on the target sheet enclosed.   The experimenter will need to be present throughout unless the sealing is entirely adequate. He then takes the unopened envelope to the second experimenter and in the presence of both the envelope is opened.   The checking is carried out independently by the two experimenters, one working from the carbon sheets and the other from the originals.   After complete agreement is reached on the results, the score totals are entered independently in the record files of each experimenter.

It is no great tax upon the intelligence of an experimental team to design or modify the standard test procedure so as to make it virtually impossible for the two experimenters, unconsciously or otherwise, to overlook errors of recording, checking, or scoring. To apply the two-experimenter practice even to GESP tests is not difficult (speaking now only of the aspect of recording) especially when the card order is recorded in advance with a copy going to each experimenter and with the percipient's responses being recorded in duplicate. In precognition tests it is as simple as with tests of clairvoyance. The comparable precaution in precognition testing is to have the selection of the target order, as well as the whole checking operation, done throughout as a *joint operation by the two experimenters* with each retaining the full score record for his own file. It is somewhat better still to arrange for duplicate records both of targets and responses and to have independent checking.

Applying the two-experimenter plan to the PK tests is somewhat more awkward because it tends to clutter up the experimental room with the presence of an additional person. Two observers recording the fall of dice creates an impression of top-heavy emphasis on results that may be disturbing to the atmosphere of the test. Where photographic recording is possible one recorder, with the film record for a second check, can provide adequate control against errors. If two recorders *can* operate without interfering with the subject, the records should be made in silence and with the record of each recorder invisible to the other during the test. This insures the independence of the two records.

D. Precautions Against Deception

A *fourth* type of requirement for sound verification might be found in the consideration of precaution against deliberate error. This is an unusual addition to scientific method, but it is called for largely because of the exceptional character of the hypotheses being tested. Also, some of the associations psi capacities have had with practices in which deception was common make it easier than in most researches to suspect that the subject might have deceived the experimenter. Accordingly, it is advantageous, if not necessary, to give special attention to this requirement.

It is true, if all three of the requirements already listed have been fully and carefully met, it would ordinarily be impossible for the subject to practice any trickery; but it is possible to add certain supplementary safeguards that would further reinforce those precautions. In precognition tests, however, no further control against fraud is needed. In clairvoyance tests, too, the complete exclusion of deception by the subject is easily managed by the use of a two-experimenter plan. In psychokinesis, likewise, if the use of a rotating cage is adopted, or any plan that eliminates the subject's handling of the dice (and, of course, he is not recording his own results), subject trickery is ruled out. With GESP and pure telepathy, precautions have to be elaborate and have to be adapted to the special needs of the experimental situation. This methodological problem is often taken too lightly; as we have said, GESP is the hardest psi-test procedure to control adequately against error, especially error due to deception.

The safeguarding of the experiment against possible irresponsibility on the part of the experimenters themselves has been made a point for discussion in parapsychology,* though it seldom is in other branches of science. This is a consequence of the revolu-

---

* In the most recent flare-up in the long controversy over parapsychology, G. R. Price (Science and the supernatural. *Science,* August 26, 1955) suggested that deliberate fraud on the part of the investigators is the explanation of experiments that cannot be attributed to error or incompetence. His article initiated a controversy that was carried on at length in the January 6, 1956 issue of *Science,* as well as in a symposium on the topic in the *Journal of Parapsychology* for December 1955.

tionary character of its findings and the novelty of the field. It is
the general practice in the sciences simply to suspend judgment
about a new finding until adequate confirmation of a given experiment has been reported by other investigators. Just how much
confirmation is needed for a discovery each may judge for himself.
It depends a great deal on how unexpected the finding is. But
under the circumstances unusual precautions have been taken in
parapsychology to add safeguards against possible error by the
experimenters themselves—error of either a deliberate or an unconscious type. That was the purpose of the two-experimenter
plan. It is not practicable, however, even in parapsychology experiments, to require more than two experimenters for a given
project, and that is where the line has been drawn. Only in a few
instances have three been assigned, but with too many managers
the investigation becomes unwieldy. The heightened apprehen-
siveness that led to such modifications, too, belonged rather to the
period of inflamed controversy which is past, and for the more
normal situation now prevailing the two-experimenter team will
give assurance of adequate protection against error, even for the
most crucial verification stage. The cautious reader may still fall
back on confirmation for further guarantees.

These four main requirements of conditions for a crucial investigation in parapsychology have been outlined in a manner
suited to the purpose of this book. Certain general practices of
research tidiness could be added that apply to every research field.
It is always wise, for instance, to draw up in advance a written plan
for a conclusive research project. Special provision should be
made at the start to meet all reasonably possible irregular con-
tingencies (e.g., what to do with cocked dice in PK, or incomplete
runs in ESP). Disposition of records, provision for duplicates, and
a program of analyses can be provided to good advantage in the
statement of design.

There might be mentioned a great deal more on the side of good
research habits. However, the scope and degree of emphasis
followed will, we believe, adequately serve the needs and aims of
most of those who wish to pursue inquiries in parapsychology with,
of course, the exception of veteran workers in the field; these latter

should already have acquired the standards and the methods appropriate to the most careful stages of a psi investigation. Those who wish to acquire a reading acquaintance with the highest standards of controlled psi testing may, for example, consult the Pratt and Woodruff report.[1] But it is well to keep in mind that every limiting condition on an experiment is a burden, and excessive use of precautions is unwarranted waste. The conditions should be calculated to fit the needs, as intelligently conceived. The conclusions, of course, depend upon the adequacy of the weakest feature, not upon an elaborate display of many precautions.

V. *Methods of Distinguishing Types of Psi*

Another level of methodology has developed in the research program in parapsychology to establish the different types of psi processes as distinguishable one from another.* For example, once telepathy and clairvoyance had been experimentally established, each under its own set of conditions, the question arose as to whether the two were, in the last analysis, experimentally distinguishable. A similar question was raised about precognition and psychokinesis. In each case, the evidence for any given type was sufficiently challenged by critical questioning to require new methods for what amounted to a re-establishment of the type concerned. A general account of these methodological distinctions will help in the appreciation of the quality of the research procedure on which the structure of parapsychology rests.

Again, it was clairvoyance that first yielded to experimental attack and permitted a distinguishing line to be drawn around its phenomena. In clairvoyance tests designed to exclude the possibility of telepathy and precognitive telepathy, it was necessary to have the trials made in such a way that not only did no one know the card order during the test, but so that even when the checking

---

* While this section is written from the point of view of the *actual development* of methods for distinguishing types of psi, the purpose is still one of presenting only a general description of methods. References to the literature will therefore not be given here, but they will be found in the later chapters in which the results of the research are discussed.

LIBRARY ST. MARY'S COLLEGE

was done no trace was left of the order in which the responses were made. Thus no one would ever know this order. In other words, the test scored the number of hits made but left no record of the order in which the calls or responses were made. Accordingly, precognitive telepathy was ruled out; no potential agent ever knew which target was for which trial when the final checking was done. This case against precognitive telepathy rests on the clairvoyance tests with matching methods, and depends on the assumption that the cards in a given pile that are laid down opposite a given key card are not identified in terms of their original positions in the pack. The issue could be investigated with somewhat better nicety by means of a clairvoyance test machine in which merely the total hits and trials are counted.

To safeguard a telepathy test against the possibility of precognitive clairvoyance was more difficult. It was necessary to avoid having any card or other objective target recorded or existing anywhere, either at the time of the test or later on. The agent or sender had to select the target mentally and, after the run was finished, to check the percipient's record from his own subjective code. To serve the agent as a random guide in selecting the target order, a shuffled pack of numbered cards or a list of random numbers might be followed; but the code which the agent used had to be one which he alone knew and which he could never record. No physical record could be allowed that could disclose the code, even by means of clairvoyance. The problem of introducing a second observer so as to make the test more reliable presented a greater difficulty. It was necessary for the agent to communicate his code to an assistant, using wholly subjective references in making his meaning clear. He had to convey his code by hints and vague clues to common memories, avoiding even an auditory stimulus that might serve as a basis for disclosure through clairvoyance. The procedure is exceedingly circuitous and perhaps not entirely logic-tight. Telepathy is the hardest of the psi types to isolate by distinctive experimental test.

The test of precognition has been successfully safeguarded against the possibility of explanation by psychokinesis by a method of selecting the target order. This method involves an extremely complex computation, starting with the throwing of dice to get a set of numbers. These numbers are involved in a routinized but complicated operation with the use of an electrical computer, ending up with a set of numbers that, by means of a fixed code, indicates the targets of the test. Everything is mechanical routine after the selection of the numbers by the throw of the dice. Although someone could, by means of PK, affect the fall of the dice that start the process of selecting the target series, he could not, in any conceivable way, produce a given set of targets by that means. The computation he would have to make to connect the dice with the end result would seem to be an impassable barrier.

The psychokinesis test itself has been safeguarded against the alternative of precognition. The supposition of the counter-theory of precognition would be that the subject or experimenter, in selecting the face of the die which is to be the target for a given set of throws, might base his choice upon precognitive awareness of the way the dice were going to fall by chance in the series to follow. That is, he would choose the face he foresaw would turn up the most frequently. It is possible to eliminate this hypothesis by simply choosing the target face by the throw of a die (see p. 62). The routine adherence to the practice of always taking the target faces in the order from one to six would leave very little room for precognition, though there is a slight advantage in the other device mentioned.

Other counter proposals have been made, including the use of the Latin Square method of determining random target sequence. This can be done to assure that the different faces will be equally represented in each subdivision of the data. If the simplest method of throwing a die to select a target is used, before the experiment is finished it is necessary to equalize the number of times each face is used as target. This requires only that the die be thrown again if a face is obtained after it has already been used as target the requisite number of times. The best evidence of PK, however, the internal decline effect known as "the quarter distribution" or QD result, is not affected by the precognition counter-hypotheses. The results had been originally collected for another purpose. (The QD analysis was a later research carried out by the Re-examination Method.)

For the most part the efforts that have been made to distinguish between the various types of psi have represented an advanced level of inquiry even for the research worker in parapsychology himself. Most of it has been done under the better controlled conditions appropriate to verification. We must remember, however, that those not primarily concerned with the advancement of parapsychology proper will not be at this stage particularly concerned with these highly refined efforts at the discriminative investigation of a specified type of psi phenomena.

In other words, the investigator who wishes to use an ESP test in some related research area need not attempt to distinguish in a thoroughgoing fashion among clairvoyance, telepathy, and precognition. For most purposes it would not make any great difference which type of psi was involved. In any case, we do not know that the types represent fundamental differences. And if they do there is no evidence yet that one type substitutes for another which the subject is attempting to use. There is no reason to think, for example, that if a subject is attempting to succeed in a clairvoyance test that he does actually achieve his results by precognitive telepathy even though the experimental conditions would allow such an alternative round-about way of response. This is not, however, to overlook the need for such clear-cut experimental distinctions as may be made.

The methods presented in the sections of this chapter, along with the supporting techniques (Part II) that implement them, are comparable in objectivity to the areas of science to which, in general, parapsychology belongs: first, psychology; and, more generally, biology. The specific techniques of investigation are naturally adapted to the phenomena to be dealt with and the conditions under which they must be studied. These were determined by the spontaneous manifestations of psi capacity that initiated the research program in parapsychology; that is to say, they were largely determined by the nature of the phenomena themselves.

The distinction between the exploratory and verification stages of research method has been strongly emphasized in this chapter in order to guide the student and research worker as quickly and effectively as possible to the stage at which he should be working. It should be pointed out, however, that for the most part it is only the advanced investigator himself who is likely to be especially concerned with verification at its most rigorous level. If our interpretation of the need for this volume is correct, it is probable that most of those concerned with actual methods, those who will undertake psi testing in one interest or another, will deal mainly with what in this chapter have been ranked as exploratory procedures. Let it be made clear, then, that there is no ranking of these methodological stages such that one can say the more rigorously controlled the test method the better. It may, in fact, be the worse if the situation calls for a free-moving, more exploratory approach. For example, in the wide range of what might be called clinical applications of psi tests, ready adaptability in method is so important that the more elaborate procedures and precautions of a crucial experiment should not even be considered.

Fortunately for parapsychology, however, some of those whose interest in psi begins as an incidental one may make first-rate discoveries that would call for further pursuit under the most advanced research design. Such an outcome is devoutly to be wished for and encouraged. If this general outline of the ways of investigating psi has been well enough presented to give an introductory picture, the inquirer, on whatever front, will be able to find or develop the plan of procedure best suited to his purpose.

The various adaptations of methods to particular uses such as clinical applications will doubtless develop many alterations; certainly as the interest in psi expands into adjacent fields, the methods will have to be adapted to fit the specialized needs. It will be advantageous, however, to maintain the same basic standards throughout and thus allow for easy comparison and interpretation of results across the boundary lines. The methods now in use will be found to adapt readily and widely without changing the basic structure.

Reference

1. PRATT, J. G., and WOODRUFF, J. L.: Size of stimulus symbols in extrasensory perception. *J. Parapsychol.*, 3:121–158, 1939.

Additional Reading

ANGIER, R. P., COBB, P. W., DALLENBACH, K. M., DUNLAP, K., FERN-
BERGER, S. W., JOHNSON, H. M., and McCOMAS, H. C.: Adequate ex-
perimental testing of the hypothesis of "extrasensory perception"
based on card-sorting. *J. Parapsychol.*, 3:28–37, 1939.
BURTT, E. A.: *Principles and Problems of Right Thinking.* New York,
Harper, 1931.
EDITORIAL: Parapsychology and scientific recognition. *J. Parapsychol.*,
16:225–232, 1952.
EDITORIAL: Rational acceptability of the case for psi. *J. Parapsychol.*,
18:184–194, 1954.
EDITORIAL: Some considerations of methods in parapsychology, *J.
Parapsychol.*, *18*:69–81, 1954.
EDITORIAL: The value of reports of spontaneous psi experiences. *J.
Parapsychol.*, *12*:231–235, 1948.
MURPHY, G.: The importance of spontaneous cases. *J. Am. Soc. Psych.
Res.*, *47*:89–103, 1953.
POPE, D. H., and PRATT, J. G.: The ESP controversy. *J. Parapsychol.*,
6:174–189, 1942.
RHINE, J. B.: *The Reach of the Mind.* New York, Sloane, 1947, pp.
154–183.
RHINE, J. B.: Impatience with scientific method in parapsychology.
J. Parapsychol., *11*:283–295, 1947.
RHINE, J. B., *et al.*: *Extrasensory Perception after Sixty Years.* New
York, Holt, 1940, pp. 22–69.
RHINE, J. B., HUMPHREY, B. M., and PRATT, J. G.: The PK effect: Spe-
cial evidence from hit patterns. III. Quarter distributions of the
half-set. *J. Parapsychol.*, 9:150–168, 1945.
RHINE, L. E.: Conviction and associated conditions in spontaneous
cases. *J. Parapsychol.*, *15*:164–191, 1951.
SOAL, S. G., and PRATT, J. G. ESP performance and target sequence.
J. Parapsychol., *15*:192–215, 1951.
The ESP symposium at the A.P.A. *J. Parapsychol.*, 2:247–272, 1938.

Chapter 3

The Facts About Psi and Its Types

W HILE we shall take for granted that the reader who has come so far as to begin this chapter will have a sufficiently open mind to consider this necessarily brief review of the case for psi, adequate references will be given for any who may wish more extensive evidence.

In presenting the facts about psi we must, of course, leave the reader to determine for himself the extent of his acceptance of them. At the same time, it is taken for granted that any accurate presentation of evidence on an important question merits attention, whatever the preconceptions of the reader. Science—we all like to think—needs and accepts no authority; its course is determined by its facts. The findings here summarized are receiving attention, however, not only because of the reliability of the evidence in support of them, but also because they are manifestly important to many departments of human interest.

After a consideration of the evidence for the establishment of psi, there will be a review of the different types of psi occurrence that have been experimentally isolated. There will be left for succeeding chapters the facts about psi in its relation to the physical world, about its psychological nature, and its relation to some of the other fields of science.

I. The Evidence for Psi

It is now safe to say—though only recently so—that the collections of spontaneous case material themselves constitute valuable evidence in support of the occurrence of psi. It is quite true that this material would not be sufficient by itself, but along with the experimental evidence it offers a very considerable amount of support to the conclusiveness of the case. Now that the spontaneous cases in the collections at different centers number in the thousands, and systematic classification and analysis of this material have been made by different workers, there emerges an impressive outline of the orderliness of the similar types of experience even though they come from widely different cultures and different periods of time. As research workers studying these reports observe the recurrence of familiar patterns of experience, each with its identifying characteristics, the characteristics turn out to be as distinctive as is the clinical case material of the physician which characterizes types of disease syndromes.[1] Accordingly, respect for this case material has grown as study has continued. It is a significant fact that each of the types of psi phenomena that have been observed and identified in the spontaneous case collections has now been demonstrated experimentally. Thus a mutual order of testimony from case study and experiment has resulted.

But psi phenomena have been under investigation for at least 75 years, and experimental work now forms the main basis of evidence. The long exposure of the problems to controversy has itself led to a great deal of research as one explorer after another tried to improve on the work of his predecessors who had failed to win scientific recognition. Studies have cropped out in a number of adjacent fields in connection with other interests as, for instance, in the study of hypnosis, among psychoanalysts and other psychiatrists, among anthropologists, and in still other fields. During the last 40 years there has been a growing interest in exploratory testing of ESP in university laboratories, mainly in departments of psychology. The great bulk of accumulated experimental evidence now available is a consequence of these scattered but numerous studies made either within the university laboratory or at least under the influence of standards set by the university researches.

The first experiment which in our judgment met the criteria for a conclusive test of ESP was one that has come to be known as the Pearce-Pratt Series. This experiment, conducted at Duke University in 1933–34,[2] was of the clairvoyance type with experimenter and subject in different buildings at least 100 yards apart. Duplicate records were kept both of the cards and of the subject's responses, one copy of each being placed in an envelope and sealed immediately following the end of the session, and the sealed envelopes being delivered to a second experimenter. The results of the series were so far above chance expectation as to be highly significant and no alternative to ESP has ever been proposed (except the vaguely implied one that it could have been fraudulently produced) that was not already anticipated and met by the experimental design. Since one phase of the experiment involved the presence of both experimenters throughout the session, conspiracy would have needed to involve all three participants. The two experimenters in this case were the present authors.

Through the succeeding years a number of other experiments followed in which the standards of control required for verification were maintained. Perhaps the most elaborately controlled of these was that published by Pratt and Woodruff[3] in 1939, about five years after the first publication of the Pearce-Pratt series. The Pratt-Woodruff series was likewise a clairvoyance experiment, and again it was conducted with the two-experimenter plan. The two experimenters operated throughout this series as checks upon each other to avoid the possibility of error in the production and recording of the results. A third member of the team played an essential part in the precautions, mainly to see that the record sheets were duly preserved and safeguarded by a system of interlocking controls. In this experiment the subjects tested were 32 volunteers. Here, too, the scoring rate was highly significant and chance as well as all the other conceivable hypotheses were ruled out, leaving only the hypothesis of ESP.

The confirmation of the case for ESP was not, however, at all confined to the Duke Laboratory. Other studies were made in other departments of psychology and elsewhere in this country as well as in Western Europe. By far the most elaborately controlled of these investigations were those conducted in London by Soal and Goldney[4] and later by Soal and Bateman.[5] These were of the GESP (general extrasensory perception) type which call for more elaborate controls, but such were the safeguards introduced by Soal and his colleagues that these studies belong within the classification of conclusive tests.

The ESP investigations by Soal and his colleagues offer evidence that is especially needed for those who are inclined to suspect that favorable ESP results may have been unduly affected by the experimenter's belief in psi. (The suspicion is not consistent with the facts.) Soal was one of the more outspoken critics of the earlier ESP investigations when he began, and repeatedly during the course of a long period of searching for ESP subjects he announced that his results were negative. It was months after his tests were completed that his attention was called to evidence of ESP in his data. This "indirect evidence" as we may call it, was, so to speak, forced upon his attention by another worker against his own anticipation. Soal had tested 160 subjects for ESP capacity and at first thought his results could be explained by chance. Another investigator, Whately Carington, meanwhile had found among his own ESP records a tendency on the part of subjects to "displace," as he called it, and to hit the target which came before or that which came after the one set up for the subject at the time.[6] When he called Soal's attention to this effect and asked him to examine his card-calling tests for displacement, Soal discovered that two of his own subjects had shown it.[7] They had not gone above chance on the target, but on the "next door" targets they scored so strikingly that even when all the necessary corrections were made the results were still statistically significant. It was this displacement effect, then, that became the main basis of the further conclusive experiments under the direction of Soal and Goldney.

Indirect evidence of various kinds was also turned up in other investigations, and all together it makes up a good part of the body of evidence of ESP. For example, in the early experiments there was evidence of a falling off of success in the runs or in the series of trials given as a block in the test situation. This decline in scoring seemed to be something of a characteristic of the test. At least it held for a considerable number of subjects in various investigations. It was at first erroneously called a fatigue curve. Jephson,[8] who first gave primary attention to decline curves, pointed out that the pioneer study of ESP by Estabrooks[9] at Harvard had shown such a decline. Now Estabrooks himself did not base his conclusions upon this effect. But when this experiment was later evaluated for the significance of its decline in scoring rate in the run, this evidence alone gave it the status of an extrachance series.[10] It was thus an incidental result unanticipated by Estabrooks and even ignored in his estimate of significance. This unexpected finding in Estabrooks' evidence would have a more telling effect upon some minds than would the obvious direct results upon which he based his own conclusions.

It might be well to turn to another branch of psi investigations for a third illustration of this indirect type of evidence. In the earlier work on psychokinesis, most of which would qualify only as exploratory by the standards of evidence presented in the preceding chapter, final verification was based upon precisely this indirect kind of proof. Although a number of experimenters had completed PK test series without suspecting that the data had any

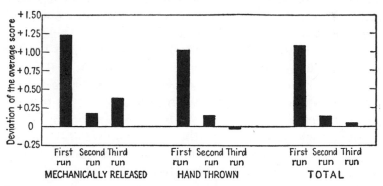

Decline in scoring rate within the set of three runs in the first series of dice-throwing tests of PK (*J. Parapsychol.*, 7:20–43, 1943).

significance beyond that shown by the total scores, when later the records were analyzed more closely in the Parapsychology Laboratory internal declines in the scoring rate became manifest.[11] These declines took the general direction that many ESP record sheets had shown—a falling off in scoring down the run; but there was also a falling off to the right as the record sheets were filled out. This gave, as a combined effect, the most pronounced decline between the upper left and the lower right quarters of the page. The analyses were carried out on records from a number of earlier PK research projects that had long been gathering dust in the files, and it was obviously an investigation of unanticipated results. But when, from the continuation of the study, confirmation emerged from one series of data to another so that finally a high order of significance was shown, the evidence of the operation of a PK function became overwhelming. It far surpassed the conclusiveness of the evidence from the general results themselves which had been anticipated by the separate investigators.

In addition to the direct evidence of adequately safeguarded experiments and the supporting evidence of widespread *indirect* psi effects, there is a third type of support for the case for psi. This evidence emerges from studies of the *relation of this capacity to other observable operations or conditions.* One of the most familiar and best established of these lawful relations is shown by Schmeidler[12] in her work on the association of ESP results with the subject's attitude toward that capacity. The subject's attitude toward ESP was registered in advance of clairvoyance tests given to students in the classroom, and it was found that those with the more negative attitude (goats) tended to score at a lower rate than those taking a more positive attitude (sheep). The sheep-goat differences in scoring average were found to be fairly consistent over many experiments, and the results added up to a highly significant block of evidence. Without concerning ourselves for the moment with the nature of the relationship, the simple objective fact that a long-continued and orderly association of scoring and attitude toward the test was shown is another indication of lawfulness.

Other evidence based on psi's relation to adjacent fields might be cited. For example, the recent ESP work of van Busschbach[13] makes a similar point in a very different setting. Van Busschbach's test of school children in the classroom has been carried out in three different general situations, in the cities of Amsterdam and Utrecht in Holland and in Durham and Burlington in North Carolina, U.S.A. Tests were designed for the fifth and sixth grades, but in Holland they were also given to pupils in the upper grades through high school. In Amsterdam only the fifth and sixth grades gave significant evidence of ESP and this held true as well when the experiment was repeated in Utrecht. Again in the U.S.A. only the fifth and sixth (of the four grades, fifth to eighth, tested) scored significantly. There seems to be some lawful relation that holds over the area of testing involved, at least as far as this particular experiment is concerned. Even at present when the psi function is little understood certain natural properties and consistencies become evident as the investigations proceed.

There is still a fourth type of contribution to the kinds of evidence of psi. This is the evidence of rational acceptability which may be especially important to the mind that is not trained to the appreciation of scientific method itself. In order to be acceptable the findings have to be made reasonable. Most of the material to be presented in the chapters that follow concerns the relations of psi to other fields of science. Such interrelations make up the rationale of the newly discovered results. Familiarity with them will give such indications as we have gleaned as to how, and how well, psi fits into the scheme of nature as currently conceived.

There are, however, some general points on this rational picture of psi that may be referred to now, especially since they are likely to be lost in the more specific treatments to follow. We have pointed out already that the experiments in parapsychology have confirmed in general what had already been suggested by the study of spontaneous cases. It is an important fact indeed that the experiments have followed and supported the main types of psi phenomena as exemplified in the experiences of everyday life. It is noteworthy, too, that as the types of capacity suggested by the spontaneous material took more definite form under experimental study, a certain pattern of orderliness within the whole field of phenomena began to emerge. We no longer had telepathy, clairvoyance, precognition, and psychokinesis as isolated phenomena. From their common qualities an essential unity could be recognized. All, for instance, occurred on a very elusive spontaneous basis, and even the best experimental efforts to regulate and control any one of the four types have thus far failed to overcome this fugitive character. Certain general psychological characteristics were found throughout the whole range, and none was limited to one area of phenomena alone. Also, just as the spontaneous cases showed no apparent limitation of time and space, so those demonstrated experimentally likewise indicate a similar independence of physical relation.

The result has been that, more than had been suspected in the early decades of parapsychology, the field of study was found to be concerned with some kind of *systematic* interaction (however unknown and nonphysical its nature) between the subject and the objective environment, a form of communication between the individual and his surroundings. In ESP and PK then there has been discovered a *system* of reaction, one that parallels the sensori-motor exchange with which the individual most commonly interacts with his physical world.

In fact, so systematic has the character of the psi function now been shown to be that it has been possible to infer the logical likelihood of a different type of phenomenon from the occurrence of one already verified. When, for instance, clairvoyance had been satisfactorily demonstrated, it was anticipated that psychokinesis should be found to occur also. The existence of a psi influence of the object upon the subject logically suggested that there should also be a reaction of the subject upon the object. The experiments in psychokinesis were introduced in this way. Likewise, from the fact that clairvoyance showed no consistent relation to space, it was inferred that it should similarly show no dependence upon time. This was the logic that led to the first precognition experiments as conducted at Duke in 1933.

As the evidence of rational consistency in the expanding knowledge of psi phenomena grows with continued research, much of the earlier unacceptable strangeness disappears. It can now be said that a fully verified case for the occurrence of psi under the limitations specified in the reports has been made and all the criteria of scientific proof have been met. While an indefinite period of further investigation will have to follow before a sufficient understanding of psi can be reached to allow an effective grasp of its nature and an application of its principles, we at least know today that the phenomena occur, that the various types of effects can be identified, and that a complex system of related findings have emerged.

We turn now to examine the evidence which differentiates these various types of psi phenomena. In doing so one change of perspective will be adopted that needs to be specified here. As we pointed out in the chapter on method, there is a great deal of difference in the standards of evidence required for the establishment of a revolutionary new finding and for the elaboration of subordinate details regarding the nature of the new phenomenon. For the establishment of psi only the highest standards of evidence —higher than those ordinarily familiar in science—could be accepted as adequate to overcome the special skepticism encountered.   But in turning attention to the distinction between types of psi phenomena we shall occasionally consider blocks of evidence that, in the establishment of the case for psi itself, would have been rated only as of good exploratory quality.   For example, a two-experimenter plan may not always have been in use in the evidence considered in the rest of the chapter, although for the most part it was.

II. The Case for Clairvoyance

As should have been expected from the simplicity of the experimental controls required, clairvoyance experiments are the easiest of all to conduct.   As a result a great many more trials have been made in testing for clairvoyance than for other types of psi phenomena.   Not only is it easier to control against the more common experimental errors such as possible sensory cues or deception by the subject, but it is also easier to eliminate any alternative hypothesis (i.e., of another type of psi) that might be applied to the data.   To rule out ordinary telepathy as familiarly conceived, it is necessary only to keep the pack of target cards inverted throughout the shuffling and testing procedure.   When eventually the cards are looked at for recording, the percipient has already recorded his responses and telepathy from the experimenter is impossible.   But after the establishment of what was at least a preliminary case for precognition, a counterhypothesis was proposed to the effect that the results of clairvoyance tests could be explained by a combination of precognition and telepathy.[14]   The percipient, instead of using clairvoyance, could look forward to the point at which the cards were recorded by the experimenter and by precognitive telepathy acquire information of the card order from him.

As soon as this alternative of precognitive telepathy was pointed out as a defect in the case for clairvoyance, the proposal was made that clairvoyance be tested with a machine that would record only the total number of trials and the total number of successes. This would eliminate the possibility of precognitive telepathy. Results giving significant evidence of clairvoyance were reported by Tyrrell,[15] who used such an apparatus in an exploratory series of experiments. The point was met, too, in another way. This was done by card-matching techniques as in the Humphrey and Pratt "chute" series.[16] In this a pack of twenty-five cards were distributed by the subject who dropped each card through an opening marked by one of the five key cards· The cards fell in five disarranged piles and the order in which they were laid down was not noticed or recorded. The experimenters, in picking up each pile for recording and checking, paid no attention to the order. Accordingly, the subject, even if he had been inclined to try precognitive telepathy, would not have had an ordered sequence of card observations which he might observe by precognition as the experimenter made his record of the cards. Even if the subject were to try to think (unconsciously) as he indicated where the first card was to be placed, "What will the experimenter find this card to be when he picks it up and looks at it?" it appears doubtful that he could forsee (by precognitive telepathy) what the card was going to be in a certain *place* and *time* and *still be free to put it there.* In any event, it would be impossible unless the experimenter were consciously or unconsciously keeping track of the cards as he looked at them. At least for the present the results from a number of the well-controlled matching series of clairvoyance tests have sufficiently satisfied the critical mind so as not to have made it seem urgent to develop a new clairvoyance test machine just to carry the matter to a further point of determination.[17] The case for the experimental demonstration of clairvoyance appears to be sufficiently clear-cut for the present requirements of the field.

III. The Problem of Telepathy

Telepathy is by far the most familiar of the different types of psi phenomena. Most of the spontaneous cases reported are open to interpretation in terms of either telepathy or clairvoyance, but as should be expected, most people having such experiences think of them as telepathic. The exchange between people is the most needed, the most interesting, and the most dramatic type of extra-sensory communication. Also, there is, in certain cultures, a philosophical inclination to regard telepathy with more favor than clairvoyance. But even though telepathy is both more popular, more familiar, and more readily acceptable even to the general scientist, it has proved to be a much more difficult phenomenon to investigate and experimentally isolate from clairvoyance.

Until the refinement of methods introduced at the Duke Labora-tory in the early thirties, there had not even been any attempt to conduct telepathy tests in a way that excluded the possibility of clairvoyance. The agent always had an object or objective record which theoretically could have served as the target just as easily as the agent's thought. The first efforts at separation of clairvoy-ance and telepathy aimed only at excluding the possibility of con-temporaneous clairvoyance, merely requiring that the agent have no object or objective record at the time the percipient was at-tempting to apprehend his thought.[18] With the signal that the subject's choice had been made, the agent was free to make his own record. But here again (as had occurred to the case for clairvoyance) the introduction of the evidence of precognition brought in a new angle of consideration.[17] Precognitive clairvoy-ance, then, had to be considered as a counterhypothesis, and this gave more difficulty than had the exclusion of simple clairvoyance. As a provision against precognitive clairvoyance it was required that the agent make *no permanent record at all* of the sequence of symbols which served as the targets for the pure telepathy test. To select the symbol sequence he could use a deck of number cards and a code which he himself had mentally devised but had not recorded (or expressed in any physical way). He could go through the test much the same as he had done in the first efforts at a pure telepathy test, with the exception that no record ever was made of individual targets. Only the record of the total run scores was recorded.

This procedure was adequate for an exploratory test but not for a conclusive one because of the need for a second experimenter or an assistânt to verify the agent's checking of the percipient's record. To get around the difficulty and obtain a second check it was necessary that the agent somehow transfer his code to another person without leaving any objective trace that could make the secret available to the percipient by clairvoyance.

This step was achieved by using a veiled method of communication that depended for its meaning upon common memories of the two persons concerned. No one else, even if he heard them, would have known what the two meant in their conversation which transferred the code unless telepathically he knew what the two persons were thinking and what their common memories had been. By this method experiments in pure telepathy were carried out with positive results by McMahan at Duke[19] and then by Soal in London.* Accordingly, the question of telepathy has, up to this stage of clarification, been answered in the affirmative. One person can apprehend another person's thought without the use of intermediate objective records. Whether this communication is from one mind to another, without a direct involvement of nervous systems which would introduce something else than direct thought transference, cannot be decided at the present stage of our knowledge of the human organism and personality. Is is not inconceivable that some clairvoyant impression of the agent's nervous system, vocal cords, or other physical accompaniment of thought may be playing a part in the so-called pure telepathy tests. It is better to say that as far as present knowledge of mind-brain relation permits an experiment to be designed on the matter, telepathy has been demonstrated between one person and another. That is where the matter will have to be left for the present.

IV. The Case for Precognition

There were two distinct grounds for inferring the occurrence of precognition in advance of any experiment to test the hypothesis. First, there had been the evidence of spontaneous cases. Throughout history and in all the case collections examples of apparent prophecy or precognition were common. When, a few years ago, L. E. Rhine[1] classified the Duke collection with respect

---

* Reference 5, pp. 255–258.

to precognition, it was found that at least 40% of the cases indicated ESP of future happenings. There was, moreover, no apparent difference in the character of these experiences other than
in the fact that the event, instead of being only remote in space,
was also in the future. While this spontaneous material was not
regarded as offering conclusive evidence, it was noteworthy that
precognition cases often made a stronger impression than instances
of contemporaneous ESP. The timing of the experience in advance of the event with which it was connected, while it allowed
greater range for coincidence, also gave more opportunity for the
communication of it and in some cases the recording, as, for example, in letters.

The second basis which made precognition predictable was in
the experimental findings on ESP. By December, 1933, when precognition was first subjected to experimental test at the Duke
Laboratory, a considerable amount of exploratory evidence had
accumulated to indicate that ESP showed no regular relations to
distance between subject and object. This experimental confirmation of the impression already given by the spontaneous case
material that distance was no limiting factor in ESP led to the
inference that the ability should not be expected to be related to
time either. In a time-space system independence of space would
have to mean comparable freedom from time. It was accordingly
anticipated that subjects would be able to predict the order of
cards prior to the shuffling.

The experimental study of precognition has gone on in a limited
way for more than 20 years; it is still an active field of inquiry
and may prove to be the most stimulating branch of psi research
for a long time to come. The first experiments involved the attempt to predict card orders in advance of hand shuffling of the
pack. When this had been found to succeed, mechanical shuffling
was then introduced to get around the possibility that hand shuffling might be influenced by ESP itself.[20] Later still it was con-
ceded as a theoretical possibility that the card shuffling by machine could be influenced by PK and thus make the resulting card
order conform to the predictions already registered. As a third
advance, then, there came the introduction of what is known as
the "weather cut."[21,22] Figures printed in temperature readings

published in the daily press were by specified rules taken and used as the basis for the cut to be made in the packs of cards used as targets. This introduced a large order of natural phenomena as an essential link—something presumed to be beyond the control of PK. The test procedure as a whole represented a complex system in itself so that the alternative of matching calls against future targets in some other way than by precognition would involve much more than exerting an influence on the weather or the thermometer. In fact, the alternative hypothesis is rather fantastic. Significant results were obtained under conditions using the weather cut and the two-experimenter plan. In the Rhine and Humphrey investigation of this problem two series were carried out, each independent of the other, with results which, while only marginally significant, supported each other.

A very considerable amount of earlier work had been done, some on the two-experimenter level, both at the Duke Laboratory[23,20] and in England (by Tyrrell,[24] Carington,[6] and Soal and Goldney[4]) all of which involve precognition; but alternative explanations do remain as theoretical possibilities in these experiments. There is no need to go over these exploratory studies in detail here.

In recent years improvements of design have been introduced to give still further assurance that any significant results obtained can be attributed only to a precognitive type of psi. A number of studies in the exploratory category have been carried through at the Duke Laboratory under these improved conditions.[25-28] The results are sufficient to encourage their continued use and sufficient to keep this challenging branch of study active. The essential advance in these studies is that the final step in the selection of the targets is a complicated calculation, done by means of an electrical computing machine. This calculation is beyond anything the human mind would be capable of doing. The routine is rigidly fixed, but of course comes up with a different set of numbers each time—numbers that in no conceivable way could have been forced to come out as they did and could only have been foreseen by true precognition.

Data of a higher order of significance than is ordinarily required may reasonably be desired for a conclusion that will have such revolutionary consequences as the establishment of precognition. Most of the parapsychology workers who followed the ESP researches and advanced through the different stages of designing precognition experiments were satisfied at the stage of the "weather cut" method of target randomization. Some at even still earlier stages thought the evidence conclusive. To those, however, to whom precognition is philosophically impossible all the evidence will still probably not be sufficient. For those who consider that the experimental work was only needed to confirm the rational expectations we have mentioned, the demands for verification have already been sufficiently met. But if the present strong indications are correct, the accumulation of evidence will go on until opposing philosophies give way, as they eventually must do under pressure from reliable experimental results.

V. The Case for Psychokinesis

The approach to psychokinesis was very similar to that leading up to the experimental study of precognition. There had, in the reports of spontaneous "psychic" experiences, been numerous instances in which some unexplainable physical effect was reported —the stopping of clocks, falling of pictures, and the like, generally associated with a crisis or tragedy involving a member of the family. The interpretation usually given by those to whom these physical effects were manifested was that some personal agency brought them about in a way that no known physical principle could account for. There was implied some direct action of mind over matter as the term psychokinesis denotes.

It would have been, however, quite as reasonable to expect some such effect as PK from a rational interpretation of ESP. Beginning with the analogy of the sensorimotor interaction between the subject and his environment in its more familiar manifestation, and having found in extrasensory perception the counterpart of sensory perception, it seemed reasonable to look for evidence of an *extramotor* response to pair off with the familiar motor response system. Or again, (using one of the familiar patterns of thought followed in all the sciences, the law of reaction) when it was established that an object can be cognized by means of ESP it seemed to follow logically that a reaction to the action should be expected to occur likewise. In other words, when an object and subject were found to interact in one direction it was anticipated there would also be an effect in the reverse direction—from the subject to the object. Accordingly at a certain stage of experimental development of the ESP work it seemed justifiable to look for PK experimentally.

Historically there had been many ineffectual efforts made to investigate claims of physical effects said to have been produced by extraphysical influences or agencies. However, the first investigation of PK by methods that lent themselves to adequate control began with the adaptation of dice-throwing as a laboratory test at Duke early in 1934.[29] After nine years of exploratory experiments the Duke Laboratory arrived at a definitive approach to the problem which meets the requirements for verification on its more advanced level. These conclusive studies (made, incidentally by the Re-examination Method) were made on the records of eighteen separate investigations carried out in, or in conjunction with, the Duke Laboratory. The individual investigations were, for the most part, different, but all of them involved the same essential operation, the subject's conscious effort to influence the fall of dice so as to make a specified face or combination of faces turn up.

It had been observed in re-examining certain PK test data that there was a tendency for the scoring to decline to the right and downward on the page as the tests proceeded. Consequently an analysis was done to check up on both of these decline tendencies in all the PK series that had been recorded in such a way that the record sheets could be divided into quarters. Then the upper left and lower right quarters were compared as the ones which were expected to show the greatest difference in scoring rates. This diagonal decline became a mark and measure of PK evidence. In the first report by Rhine and Humphrey[11] the quarter distribution or QD of the eighteen series was given as one composite value. The evidence was highly significant of a reliable trend which could not conceivably be attributed to any other factor than a mental one having to do with the direct influencing of the dice. A later study was made that was in every respect independently confirmatory. It was based upon eight of the eighteen series in which

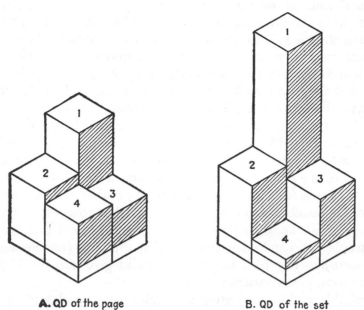

A. QD of the page B. QD of the set

I. HIGH-DICE AND LOW-DICE SERIES

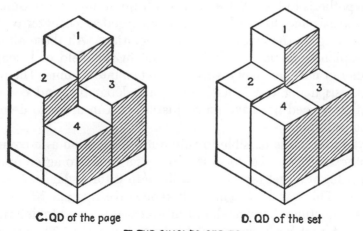

C. QD of the page D. QD of the set

II. THE SINGLES SERIES

Quarter distribution (QD) of hits on the record page and in the set. This gives a further breakdown than is mentioned in the text, showing two main subdivisions of the PK data. (See Glossary for terms "singles," etc.)

smaller units of recording were used, units called half-sets.[30] These were also given the QD analysis and the composite diagonal decline obtained showed once again an extraordinarily high order of statistical significance. In a subsequent report the independent analysis of the same material by Pratt[31] exemplified the fact that the case now has the special advantage that the entire analytic study is repeatable by any qualified examiner.

But there is the rather hair-splitting argument that perhaps the subjects in their PK performance may be exercising precognition of the way the dice are going to fall by chance, especially since the procedure in a number of the experimental series allowed the subjects to choose for a given session (or set or other unit) whichever one of the possible targets he preferred for that occasion. Perhaps, the argument ran, the subject (or the experimenter) precognized the whole series and made some mental appraisal (unconsciously, of course) as to which target face would give him the highest scores for a given session or set.

Probably nothing can give the reader a better idea of the extremes which the demands for acceptable experimental design reach in parapsychology than this use of precognition as a counter-hypothesis to PK. Yet it is only a little, if any, less reasonable than the extremes to which PK has been urged as a counterhypothesis bearing on the evidence for precognition. All these alternative explanations need to be ruled out in this field of research, whether or not they may involve a good counter claim. The main hypothesis under test is itself new and debatable, and counterhypotheses need not have much justification in order to demand full consideration.

At any rate, it is possible to rule out precognition as a counterhypothesis to PK. To do so it is necessary only to agree upon a rigid order of target face and to adhere to it throughout the series of tests. This was done in more than one investigation.[32,33] Better still, as sometimes happened, the subject was allowed to determine his own target for a given unit by throwing a die. Then, if precognition entered into it, it would have to be through the PK influence on this die.[34] At least one investigation has been made with the use of an elaborate design (Latin Square method) of selecting the target sequence by which is excluded the step-by-step choice of target on which the counterhypothesis depends.[35] But the best answer to the precognition counterhypothesis is given by the QD analyses already described. It adds something too that these were made on the data long after the tests were finished. These give the best evidence of PK, and they show that the hits were not a *selected chance distribution* as the precognition counterhypothesis assumes.

In general it can be said that a good case has been made for the occurrence of PK as an aspect of psi. It is the newest of the distinguishable psi phenomena and as a result much of the research has been concentrated in the Duke Laboratory, just as it has with precognition. Among the important independent confirmations that have, however, been carried out in other centers of research is that by McConnell, Snowden, and Powell of the University of Pittsburgh, in which a completely mechanized operation was involved, including the photographic recording of the fall of the dice.[36]

References

1. RHINE, L. E.: Frequency of types of experience in spontaneous precognition. *J. Parapsychol.*, 18:93–123, 1954.
2. RHINE, J. B., and PRATT, J. G.: A review of the Pearce-Pratt distance series of ESP tests. *J. Parapsychol.*, 18:165–177, 1954.
3. PRATT, J. G., and WOODRUFF, J. L.: Size of stimulus symbols in extrasensory perception. *J. Parapsychol.*, 3:121–158, 1939.
4. SOAL, S. G., and GOLDNEY, K. M.: Experiments in precognitive telepathy. *Proc. Soc. Psychical Res.*, 47:21–150, 1943.
5. SOAL, S. G., and BATEMAN, F.: *Modern Experiments in Telepathy.* New Haven, Yale, 1954.
6. CARINGTON, W.: Experiments on the paranormal cognition of drawings. *Proc. Soc. Psychical Res.*, 46:34–151, 1940. Published simultaneously in *J. Parapsychol.*, 4:1–134, 1940.
7. SOAL, S. G.: Fresh light on card guessing—some new effects. *Proc. Soc. Psychical Res.*, 46:152–198, 1940.
8. JEPHSON, I: Evidence for clairvoyance in card-guessing. *Proc. Soc. Psychical Res.*, 38:223–268, 1929.
9. ESTABROOKS, G. H.: A contribution to experimental telepathy. *Bull. Boston Soc. Psychic Res.*, Bulletin V, 1927.

10. RHINE, J. B.: *The Reach of the Mind*. New York, Sloane, 1947,
    p. 170.
11. RHINE, J. B., and HUMPHREY, B. M.: The PK effect: Special evi-
    dence from hit patterns. I. Quarter distributions of the page.
    J. Parapsychol., 8:18–60, 1944.
12. SCHMEIDLER, G. R., and MURPHY, G.: The influence of belief and
    disbelief in ESP upon ESP scoring level. *J. Exper. Psychol.*,
    36:271–276, 1946.
13. VAN BUSSCHBACH, J. G.: An investigation of ESP between teacher
    and pupils in American schools. *J. Parapsychol.*, 20:71–80, 1956.
14. CARINGTON, W.: *Telepathy: An Outline of Its Facts, Theory, and
    Implications*. London, Methuen, 1945, pp. 91–92.
15. TYRRELL, G. N. M.: The Tyrrell apparatus for testing extrasensory
    perception. *J. Parapsychol.*, 2:107–118, 1938.
16. HUMPHREY, B. M., and PRATT, J. G.: A comparison of five ESP test
    procedures. *J. Parapsychol.*, 5:267–292, 1941.
17. RHINE, J. B.: Telepathy and clairvoyance reconsidered. *J. Para-
    psychol.*, 9:176–193, 1945.
18. RHINE, J. B.: *Extrasensory Perception*. Boston, Bruce Humphries,
    1934.
19. MCMAHAN, E. A.: An experiment in pure telepathy. *J. Parapsy-
    chol.*, 10:224–242, 1946.
20. RHINE, J. B.: Experiments bearing upon the precognition hypoth-
    esis. III. Mechanically selected cards. *J. Parapsychol.*, 5:1–57,
    1941.
21. RHINE, J. B.: Evidence of precognition in the covariation of
    salience ratios. *J. Parapsychol.*, 6:111–143, 1942.
22. RHINE, J. B., and HUMPHREY, B. M.: A confirmatory study of sali-
    ence in precognition tests. *J. Parapsychol.*, 6:190–219, 1942.
23. HUTCHINSON, L.: Variations of time intervals in pre-shuffle card-
    calling. *J. Parapsychol.*, 4:249–270, 1940.
24. TYRRELL, G. N. M.: Further experiments in extrasensory percep-
    tion. *Proc. Soc. Psychical Res.*, 44:99–168, 1936.
25. MANGAN, G. L.: Evidence of displacement in a precognition test.
    J. Parapsychol., 19:35–44, 1955.
26. OSIS, K.: Precognition over time intervals of one to thirty-three
    days. *J. Parapsychol.*, 19:82–91, 1955.
27. NIELSEN, W.: An exploratory precognition experiment. *J. Parapsy-
    chol.*, 20:33–39, 1956.
28. NIELSEN, W.: Mental states associated with success in precogni-
    tion. *J. Parapsychol.*, 20:96–109, 1956.

29. RHINE, J. B., and RHINE, L. E.: The psychokinetic effect: I. The first experiment. *J. Parapsychol.*, 7:20–43, 1943.
30. RHINE, J. B., HUMPHREY, B. M., and PRATT, J. G.: The PK effect: Special evidence from hit patterns. III. Quarter distributions of the half-set. *J. Parapsychol.*, 9:150–168, 1945.
31. PRATT, J. G.: A reinvestigation of the quarter distribution of the (PK) page. *J. Parapsychol.*, 8:61–63, 1944.
32. PRATT, J. G., and WOODRUFF, J. L.: An exploratory investigation of PK position effects. *J. Parapsychol.*, 10:197–207, 1946.
33. DALE, L. A.: The psychokinetic effect: The first A.S.P.R. experiment. *J. Am. Soc. Psychical Res.*, 40:123–151, 1946.
34. HUMPHREY, B. H.: Simultaneous high and low aim in PK tests. *J. Parapsychol.*, 11:160–174, 1947.
35. THOULESS, R. H.: A report on an experiment on psychokinesis with dice, and a discussion of psychological factors favouring success. *Proc. Soc. Psychical Res.*, 49:107–130, 1949–1952.
36. McCONNELL, R. A., SNOWDEN, R. J., and POWELL, K. F.: Wishing with dice. *J. Exper. Psychol.*, 50:269–275, 1955.

Additional Reading

A digest and discussion of some comments on: Telepathy and Clairvoyance Reconsidered. *J. Parapsychol.*, 10:36–50, 1946.
BIRGE, W. R.: A new method and an experiment in pure telepathy. *J. Parapsychol.*, 12:273–288, 1948.
MUNDLE, C. W. K.: The experimental evidence for PK and precognition. *Proc. Soc. Psychical Res.*, 49:61–78, 1949–52.
MURPHY, G.: Needed: Instruments for differentiating between telepathy and clairvoyance. *J. Am. Soc. Psych. Res.*, 42:47–49, 1948.
NASH, C. B.: Psychokinesis reconsidered. *J. Amer. Soc. Psychical Res.*, 45:62–68, 1951.
RHINE, J. B.: Precognition reconsidered. *J. Parapsychol.*, 9:264–277, 1945.
RHINE, J. B.: The psychokinetic effect: A review. *J. Parapsychol.*, 10:5–20, 1946.
SCHMEIDLER, G.: Position effects as psychological phenomena. *J. Parapsychol.*, 8:110–123, 1944.

LIBRARY ST. MARY'S COLLEGE

Chapter 4

Psi and the Physical World

I. First the Facts

For the last two decades it has been possible to define the field of parapsychology in a clear-cut fashion as one that deals with phenomena not explainable by physical principles. There is a great part of mental life that may or may not be nonphysical, but parapsychology at the present stage is not concerned with effects for which the interpretation is ambiguous. In order to be considered as parapsychological the phenomena must be demonstrably nonphysical. That is, they must occur under conditions that clearly eliminate the types of operation known as physical. In their spontaneous occurrence the phenomena of parapsychology appear to defy physical explanation and when examined experimentally they can be proved to be beyond the reach of physical explanation. (We need hardly add that we are using terms and concepts in their current meanings; any other would be too conjectural for scientific use.)

It is a matter of history that the founding of this branch of science derived its initiative from the interest many scholars of the nineteenth century felt in discovering whether all nature was, as was assumed in the growing philosophy of materialism, a purely physical system. Are there mental processes that are not a part of the world of physics? In their search for an answer to this question the founders of parapsychology were looking for possible nonphysical phenomena in nature that might be scientifically observed and described.

A. Distance and ESP

To these early explorers reports of spontaneous thought-transference occurring between individuals separated by great distances made the strongest appeal of all the current psychic claims. The apparent meeting of mind with mind in spite of intervening physical barriers would, if it could be reliably established as a natural phenomenon, argue strongly against a wholly physicalistic interpretation of human personality. The first step undertaken, that of collecting accounts of such spontaneous happenings (which came to be called telepathy) not only deepened the impression among scholars that a valid principle was operating in such cases; it strengthened the suggestion that this operation was completely independent of any known physical condition. It seemed to make no difference whether the percipient and the agent were separated by short distances or by very long ones, so far as either the frequency or the vividness of the experiences was concerned.

When, after some decades of introductory inquiries, better controlled and more systematic investigations were undertaken, the distances that were introduced, often incidentally, did not seem to affect the results in any regular way. In some experiments there were higher rates of success at the shorter and in others at the longer distances.

When the Pearce-Pratt series of ESP tests introduced a comparison of distances in the Duke experiments, the scoring rate for the long distance tests (involving distances of 100 and of 250 yards) was about 30 per cent when chance expectancy was 20 per cent.[1] Earlier work by the same subject (with the cards within arm's length) had averaged approximately 32 per cent in comparably large series of runs. In the Pearce-Pratt series at 100 yards his scoring rose for the first experiment consisting of 300 trials to an average of 40 per cent, but a careful study indicates that there were important psychological differences in the timing and the preparation for this series that gave it precedence over the earlier short-distance work. When later on at a distance of 250 yards he scored only 27 per cent, it was very evident in the scoring irregularities that psychological factors were again influencing the rate of success.

The Pearce-Pratt series was the first definite experimental confirmation of the general impression given by spontaneous experiences that psi operates without showing any recognizable rela-

tionship to distance. The more complex theoretical question as
to whether there is *any* relationship, direct or otherwise, between
psi and space, is a different matter which must be left for a more
advanced stage of psi research.

A number of exploratory investigations as well as a few
experiments of the more conclusive type (represented by the
Pearce-Pratt series) continued to deal with comparisons of distances in ESP tests. We will omit a series carried out by Riess[2]
which reports the most successful scoring rate on record (over
72 per cent) because there was no short distance test made to
compare with the 400 yards over which the experiment was conducted. Here and there an exceptional subject was willing to perform at a long distance, as in the Turner-Ownbey GESP series
at Duke,[3] in which approximately 40 per cent success was obtained
in 200 trials at 250 miles as compared to a 31 per cent success at
short distance. Large group tests were conducted in which subjects located over a wide geographical area attempted to identify
cards or other target material centrally located. Among these
was a series by Whately Carington in England[4] and one under the
direction of R. W. George at Tarkio College, Missouri.[5] The
evidence of ESP from these series shows no recognizable direct
relation between results and distance. Scoring success does vary
widely, but it is evidently determined by other conditions, most
probably psychological. Regardless of the distance involved, the
better oriented subjects stand out; for instance, groups located in
some active research center have had more success than newly-
formed groups.

The longest distance over which systematic experiments have
been conducted was that between Zagreb, Yugoslavia, and Durham, North Carolina.[6] For a part of this experiment a group of
ten subjects at the Parapsychology Laboratory worked on target
cards set up by Dr. Karlo Marchesi at Zagreb, but for the major
part of the series Dr. Marchesi attempted to identify the order of
cards set up at the Duke Laboratory. This experiment was
handled as a two-experimenter operation with full precautions.
The occurrence of marginally significant results at this very long
distance was of value in the appraisal of distance as a hypothetical factor. While testing himself, prior to the long distance ex-

periments, Dr. Marchesi scored at a much higher rate than in the long distance test. In later tests performed in the Duke Laboratory he was unable to score appreciably above chance average.[7] The factors most likely to be responsible for these differences are the topic of the succeeding chapter, the psychology of psi. (Just as the book is going to press a report has been published on a short but statistically significant series between Durham and Mufulira, Northern Rhodesia.[8])

No nicer comparison of distance has been made than that of Soal and Bateman[9] in England, in which their subject, Mrs. Stewart, participated during a visit to Brussels. Thus they were able to continue at a distance of approximately 200 miles experiments similar to those that previously had been conducted with Mrs. Stewart in the room adjoining that of the sender. The fact that the scoring rate (approximately 28 per cent) continued at the same level regardless of the distance confirmed all the previously accumulated evidence that psi is not directly related to the distance separating the subject from the target.

B. ESP and Time

As the preceding chapter explained, the fact that psi seemed to show no relation to space affords a basis for expecting it not to be related to time either. If it were nonphysical in its spatial relation, it should be nontemporal too. The argument was fully in line with the well-known fact that spontaneous psi occurrences have always seemed to transcend time limits as freely as they have crossed the boundaries of space.

The argument, of course, works both ways. No better experiment could have been found to put the hypothesis of the nonphysical character of psi to test than one designed to see whether the ability could be used to respond to events beyond the present.

The evidence for precognition has been outlined in the preceding chapter. Taking into account the large background of evidence of ESP now on record, along with the indications of the independence of ESP from spatial limitations, we may consider the case for precognition as reasonably conclusive. The investigations will, of course, continue and if the case is sound the future will bring further confirmation. Science achieves no absolute certainties; but the degree of probability now applying to the case for precognition is on a par with many a major working concept in the various sciences. The arresting aspect of precognition, however, would seem to be not the question of the strength of the experimental evidence but rather the difficulty of finding an acceptable rationale for so revolutionary a principle.

But while nothing would appear to be so crucially definitive on the question of whether psi processes are really nonphysical as would the case for precognition, it is reassuring also to remember all the other evidence, too. If precognition had not lent itself to investigation and we had no data on it, there would still be a good case for the nonphysical character of psi phenomena.

C. Other Evidence of Nonphysicality

Perhaps the most rationally reassuring of all the types of evidence of the nonphysical nature of psi is the range of target material on which it is capable of functioning; that is, the range of stimuli or starting points with which it can deal (and for which some physical theory of intermediation would have to be provided). Consider, for example, the range of objects and objective conditions of target object in clairvoyance experiments and spontaneous experiences. Most commonly these are cards printed with ink, but it apparently does not matter at which angle the cards are located with respect to the subject nor how close together they are with other cards of the pack; that is, a solid pack may serve as the target with the cards all lying together in a box. Obviously, too, there is no illumination in such a case so that the familiar visual image could not be obtained from the card, and any physical or chemical difference in the card surface could not be detected by the subject under the test conditions. At the other extreme, in the pure telepathy experiments the mere thought of the card symbol by the agent is sufficient to serve as the target. And in addition, if one considers the precognition tests, the position of the card at a certain place in the pack at a certain future time will serve as the target.

The complexity of the target from a physical point of view is even greater when we consider that ESP is necessary in PK experiments too. If the falling dice are to be influenced so that the target face or combination is to be favored in the results, it is necessary to suppose that some other perception than that of the senses must direct this influence exerted upon them. In most experiments the dice fall too rapidly for visual perception to follow. In other experiments the subject does not actually see the dice at the time of release. Sometimes the dice are thrown in considerable numbers at one time so that the eye cannot follow the

Dice used for comparison of size, density, and shape of objects in PK tests, and cup used for hand-throwing.

complete movements with sufficient clarity to allow the intelligent direction of a causal influence through PK. Accordingly, we must suppose an extrasensory aspect to the PK operation—one that operates too fast for sensorimotor reaction time. ESP itself could only function in such a case by operating on something else than a physical type of causality. There would have to be intelligent purpose as an essential part of the PK influence.

PK offers other difficulties of interpretation in terms of physical principles. Exploratory efforts have been made to test the effect of distance on PK. Among these the work of Nash and Richards[10] stands out as having the best design. It yielded results which show that PK could function over a distance of 25 yards without apparent interference. Similarly, and likewise on the exploratory level of testing, it has been found repeatedly in the Duke experiments that such physical conditions as are represented in the number of dice released at a single throw, the size and density of the dice, the sharpness of corners, do not show any dependable relation to scoring results; that is, there does not seem to be any limiting physical effect from the differences mentioned. It is well to emphasize the tentative nature of these explorations until they have been more widely verified or until the investigation has been carried out on an even more crucial level. The results thus far obtained, however, are within the scope of what would have been expected from the general evidence of psi in relation to physics. But the question of the outer bounds of physical limitations in PK ought now to be investigated on a more exhaustive scale.

For that matter more investigation on the exploratory level, too, is needed. If the operation of PK should have *no* physical limitation, parapsychology would prove to be a more fundamentally revolutionary science than has yet been anticipated even by its own representatives. But there may be such limits; and if so, they should be discoverable. There may be, for that matter, limits to the extent of time over which precognition can function or even limitations to the space ESP can encompass. Now, however, our purpose is to present the known facts; and thus far no limits have been reached. That does not imply there are none; rather, the rational inclination within our present framework of thought is to expect that *some* limitations will eventually be discovered.

II. And Then the Implications

A. Psychophysical Distinctions

Parapsychologists are sometimes called dualists, meaning, of course, that they recognize two kinds of reality, mental and physical. In most scientific circles of today this philosophical position is an unpopular one. But the philosophical term dualism does not apply to a conclusion reached as a result of experimental science. Many areas of science involve some line of differentiation (for example, that between wave phenomena and particle data in modern physics), but the distinction between two aspects of a phenomenon does not constitute a dualism. The question of whether or not the operation of psi shows any reliable relation to known physical law is not a matter of interpretation. It has been brought into experimental focus and is now only a question of the facts themselves. For those who are students of science to the extent of taking their facts seriously and adjusting their philosophy to them, no doubt remains that a certain *relative duality* of aspects of nature is involved. A valid distinction has been drawn, a limited division of nature has, on the descriptive level, been discovered and verified, but these facts do not justify any theory of absolute dualism. Parapsychology stops with the facts it has established.

The establishment of the nonphysical nature of psi as a simple scientific fact does, however, make a profound difference indeed to other areas of inquiry and application—for example, to the theory of the organism, the basic nature of personality, and the larger concept of man's place in the natural order. Moreover, such a distinction between psi and physics has far-reaching importance beyond the borders of science, wherever the nature of man is an important consideration. Within the more fundamental confines of science itself the two aspects of reality now distinguished appear for the present at least to constitute areas whose interrelations themselves present new territory for the long future to explore. This longer view brings us, even in parapsychology, to a novel emphasis—in appearance almost a reversal—an emphasis indicated in the next title, on the integration of psi with the physical order of the universe.

B. Psychophysical Interaction and the Unity of Nature

The scientist will in due time be just as interested as the philosopher in the question of how these different areas of reality can interact. What do these areas have in common that can allow the exchange between them? An energy exchange has to be supposed, one that in ESP can convey information and in the PK tests do work. For the time being let it be called psychical or mental energy, leaving for a later stage of research an account of its peculiar properties. Most of the energies now recognized were at one stage as mysterious as this one. But although the concept of a mental energy is a comparatively old one, it is only through parapsychology that it has received scientific attention and been brought under actual experimental attack.

To make sense in the present situation, this mental energy would have to be one that does not stimulate the sense organs. There are already known energies in the same category. Second, such an imperceptible energy would have to be convertible to other energy states which would be perceptible to the senses. There are many known energies that are recognizable only through such translation or conversion. These are facts of familiar elementary physics. The only unique feature of this psychical energy lies in the fact that it functions without any restrictive relation (yet known) to space-time-mass criteria. But that is only to say again that such energy is not physical, since the space-time-mass criteria are the defining concepts of that field.

Impossible? No, the shrewd observer out on the frontier of physical knowledge would be the last to reject the idea of a natural mental energy. At any rate, there is now a large body of experimental fact that requires the inference of an effective principle which does not display space-time-mass properties and does not affect the sense organs. The formulation of the hypothesis of a specific energy is only a modest beginning. If the hypothesis is correct, there should be ways of verifying its validity.

Ideally, the attack upon the problem of psychophysical causation presented by psi phenomena should be considered as much an invitation and challenge to physical scientists (including physiologists) as it is to the parapsychologists. In this subject-object relation the *object* obviously means something—plays some part. The solution of the problem should lead into a causative relation extending beyond the range of knowledge of physics today. It is too early yet to say whether the field of physics will move its frontiers and adjust its concepts more quickly than that of psychology has; but for one, as for the other, it should be only a matter of recognizing the facts and having time to adjust to them. The case for psi is logically an experimental refutation of the mechanistic philosophy of nature that has become well nigh universal today in all the sciences. It exerts much the same influence on the educated mind, in preventing it from observing and considering anything that challenges mechanism, as in medieval times the supernaturalistic philosophy of that day did upon the new observations in nature that challenged its supremacy. The tendency of an existing belief to control thought is manifest not merely in the religions but in the sciences as well.

The reason for dwelling on this implication of the nonphysicality of psi is that it is a part of the scientific research itself to become aware of and deal effectively with the resistances that have to be overcome in the progressive acceptance of research findings. The methods used in the laboratory to produce results may well be vain unless methods are also developed by which to meet and change the philosophical attitude that prevents acceptance of the facts, for it condemns experimental effort to futility or at least to long and indefinite periods of being ignored. The parapsychologist has to recognize that along with his difficulties in establishing his findings in the laboratory goes the more formidable one awaiting him outside the laboratory door; that of establishing his conclusions in a way effective enough to overcome the ready-made and determined rejection of his case regardless of the scientific quality of his work. For those who have the inclination to look, an extensive literature of controversy over the findings of parapsychology exists. It will enlighten the interested reader as to the length to which even today resistance to revolutionary discovery can go and scientific progress be impeded.[3,11,12]

But once the distinction of psi as a nonphysical function is clear to modern science, the fact will automatically open a fresh new frontier of exploration into the deeper unifying connection between psi and physics. Even as we distinguish them, we concede that logically there has to be a basic underlying integration. The very interaction that makes the demonstration of psi possible shows at the same time that in this demonstration there must be a fundamental unifying principle! The bridge of common proper-

ties and interacting processes we shall one day find will be the
fruits of tomorrow's researches, when the controversies of today
over theories of man's extraphysical nature are stilled. A fuller
view of the place of man in nature with respect to the physical
world is the higher goal toward which parapsychology is leading.
It will be a constructive sequel to the distinctions of the present
stage.

References

1. RHINE, J. B., and PRATT, J. G.: Review of the Pearce-Pratt distance
   series of ESP tests. *J. Parapsychol.*, *18*:165–177, 1954.
2. RIESS, B. F.: Further data from a case of high scores in card-
   guessing. *J. Parapsychol.*, *3*:79–84, 1939.
3. RHINE, J. B., PRATT, J. G., STUART, C. E., SMITH, B. M., and GREEN-
   WOOD, J. A.: *Extrasensory Perception After Sixty Years.* New
   York, Holt, 1940, pp. 416–417.
4. CARINGTON, W.: Experiments on the paranormal cognition of drawings. *Proc. Soc. Psychical Res.*, *46*:34–151, 1940.
5. RHINE, J. B.: The effect of distance in ESP tests. *J. Parapsychol.*,
   1:172–184, 1937.
6. McMAHAN, E. A., and RHINE, J. B.: A second Zagreb-Durham ESP
   experiment. *J. Parapsychol.*, *11*:244–253, 1947.
7. McMAHAN, E. A., and BATES, E. K., JR.: Report of further Marchesi
   experiments. *J. Parapsychol.*, *18*:82–92, 1954.
8. OSIS, K.: ESP over a distance of seventy-five hundred miles. *J.
   Parapsychol.*, *20*:229–232, 1956.
9. SOAL, S. G., and BATEMAN, F.: *Modern Experiments in Telepathy.*
   New Haven, Yale, 1954, pp. 303–308.
10. NASH, C. B., and RICHARDS, A.: Comparison of two distances in PK
    tests. *J. Parapsychol.*, *11*:269–282, 1947.
11. POPE, D. H., and PRATT, J. G.: The ESP controversy. *J. Parapsy-
    chol.*, *6*:174–189, 1942.
12. The controversy in *Science* over ESP. *J. Parapsychol.*, *19*:236–271,
    1955.

Additional Reading

BROAD, C. D.: The relevance of psychical research to philosophy, in
Religion, Philosophy and Psychical Research. New York, Harcourt,
1953, pp. 7–26.

CHARI, C. T. K.: Quantum physics and parapsychology. *J. Parapsychol.*, 20:166–183, 1956.

EDITORIAL: Parapsychology and dualism. *J. Parapsychol.*, 9:225–228, 1945.

HOFFMAN, B.: ESP and the inverse square law. *J. Parapsychol.*, 4:149–152, 1940.

JORDAN, P.: Reflections on parapsychology, psychoanalysis, and atomic physics. *J. Parapsychol.*, 15:278–281, 1951.

McCONNELL, R. A.: Physical or nonphysical? *J. Parapsychol.*, 11:111–117, 1947.

MURPHY, G.: Psychical research and the mind-body relation. *J. Am. Soc. Psychical Res.*, 40:189–207, 1946.

RHINE, J. B.: The science of nonphysical nature. *J. Philosophy*, 51:801–810, 1954.

RUSH, J. H.: Some considerations as to a physical basis of ESP. *J. Parapsychol.*, 7:44–49, 1943.

WALKER, R.: Parapsychology and dualism. *Scient. Month.*, 79:1–9, 1954.

WASSERMAN, G. D.: An outline of a field theory of organismic form and behavior, in *Ciba Foundation Symposium on Extrasensory Perception.* Boston, Little, 1956, pp. 53–72.

Chapter 5

The Psychology of Psi

T HE SCIENCE that deals with persons as distinct from impersonal substances, forces, or bodies is called psychology just as the study of living organisms as distinguished from the inanimate is called biology. The characteristic that most distinguishes personal agency or behavior from an impersonal operation has not yet been successfully defined in terms of psychology. Consequently, it is still not clear in more than superficial terms just how the field of psychology is to be marked off from the rest of the studies of nature. Under the influence of the trend in science towards a mechanistic philosophy the natural effort has been to try to make psychology in effect a branch of physics. However, the discoveries concerning psi, in showing that persons are capable of certain nonphysical functions, have provided psychology with at least one fundamental distinction between a person and an impersonal thing. How far this distinguishing character extends throughout the entire structure of the personality is a matter for further study, but even at a minimal valuation it has won for psychology a scientific claim to its own distinct area of reality. Unlike all the other branches of science, it has been experimentally proved to have operations that do not yield to physical explanation.

We should expect, in view of the significance of psi for a theory of man's nature, that its position would become a more central one in general psychology as recognition of the reality of psi extends within that profession. The shift may come about slowly, but if it should require a long time, that would in itself give some measure of how profound an alteration in current thought was involved. At all events, when the eventual stage of complete recognition of psi is reached it can hardly fail to bring about a major revolution in the larger field, so fundamental is the new concept of man introduced.

The psychological study of psi has developed only comparatively recently. Naturally more attention was initially given to the establishment of the occurrence of psi and to the differentiation of the types of psi phenomena than to studying the conditions that might affect them. Even so, a considerable accumulation of psychological facts has been made, one that is already too great for review in a single chapter. Accordingly, we shall be able to take up only the main topics in the survey that follows—the questions of how normal psi is, what role it plays in the personality, and what conditions affect its demonstration.

I. Psi is Normal

Some of the early nineteenth century observers who gave attention to psi phenomena associated them with mental abnormality. The phenomena first came under professional study in connection with hypnotism or its forerunner, mesmerism. Thus psychiatry in its beginnings was linked with the odd occurrences that have come to be known as ESP.[1] Just as hypnosis was for a time erroneously attributed to the neurotic condition known as hysteria, so capacities such as clairvoyance and thought-transference were attributed to the mesmeric or hypnotic state as artificial products induced in minds that were something less than normal and healthy.[2]

A. Psi Is Not Abnormal

Hypnosis became in time more or less clearly distingished from its early association with the abnormal, and ESP phenomena, too, came to be recognized apart from the hypnotic state. However, there still remained the question whether it is perfectly healthy or normal to have spontaneous psi experiences or to be able to demonstrate psi under experimental conditions. But the answer has developed fairly clearly in recent years that psi is a normal process and is no more closely related to psychopathology than is any other mental function.

This answer is based first on the large body of evidence now available as the result of the study of spontaneous case material. The case analyses have revealed no indication of any tie-up between mental illness and proneness to psi experience. If any such relationship existed the explorer working with spontaneous cases of psi would have been quick to pick it up in his search for clues to principles. Furthermore, the mental hospital has not turned out to be the place to go in search of outstanding psi performers. Although many psychiatrists themselves have been alert to the occurrence of apparent psi experiences in their patients, they have not discovered among their patients any outstanding performers or even noted any special proneness to spontaneous parapsychical experiences.

The tendency of some sick minds to fabricate a belief that they are being controlled and persecuted by means of telepathy or some related ability exercised by supposed enemies comes under the heading of delusion. It has no bearing on the relation of psi to psychopathology. Not only have these beliefs in telepathic persecution not been found to have any basis; in the ESP tests given them the individuals concerned have not in any case so far shown outstanding telepathic ability.

Fortunately the experimental methods have been sufficiently adaptable (though far from perfectly so) to the clinical situation in the hospital to permit a fair amount of exploratory work to be carried out on different classifications of the mentally ill.[3,4] While some of these investigations have yielded extrachance results, the results have not been outstanding as compared to the general population. It is quite conceivable that more striking results would be obtained from patients in mental hospitals if a psi test better suited to the bedside situation could be developed. But thus far no outstanding performers have been found in the mental hospitals; and the search has been rather extensive. There is no reason, then, to think that mental illness favors either the spontaneous or the experimental manifestation of psi.

B. Psi Test Performance and General Adjustment

A considerable amount of exploratory psi testing has been done on groups of subjects from the normal population, especially with groups of college students, in connection with accompanying estimates of adjustment, mental health, or neurotic tendency. The trend in the comparisons made has rather generally associated higher psi-test scoring with better adjustment.[5-7]   So far as a survey of this type of evidence goes it would indicate that the better the mental health of a subject the more likely he is to contribute to *positive* scoring in ESP tests.   So we may say again that the research results, as far as they go, have indicated no relation between parapsychology and psychopathology.   The parapsychical is not likely to be psychopathological.

C. Psi and Intelligence

It is worth a brief paragraph to summarize the researches that have been done to see whether psi is linked with intelligence. The answer seems to be that it is neither more nor less likely to be manifested by persons whose intelligence is above par than by those below.   The basis for these studies is extensive enough to permit such a general statement, even though the work has all been done on the exploratory level.   The indications are that individuals on the level of the feeble-minded can perform successfully in ESP tests when the tests are adapted to their needs, but they do not yield outstanding results.[8]   There is no evidence that the proper place to search for high performance is in the institutions for the feeble minded.   There is, on the other hand, some experimental evidence—enough to warrant further inquiry— that intelligence differences at the college level show slight positive correlation with ESP test scores.[9]   This apparent linkage may be due to better adaptability to the test situation on the part of the more intelligent.   There is no adequate ground as yet to think that psi varies with intelligence as such.

D. Is Psi Normal Equipment for Man?

There is space for considering one more of the numerous meanings of the word "normal."   We have already considered normality from the point of view of mental health and intelligence.   Let us now ask whether psi is a natural function of personality—whether it is part of the normal equipment of the individual, so that a lack of it would be abnormal.   Obviously a precise answer to this question would call for the investigation of too large a sample of the human species for the present stage of parapsychology.   Any answer given now must be an inference from a comparatively

small section of the whole. It will have to be from a very spotty
selection of data, too, because no systematic study of the distribution of psi capacity over the human race as a whole has ever
been undertaken. Such a survey based on proper sampling may
be long in coming. Any judgment made now will have to depend
upon only incidental samplings and the results taken for what they
are worth.

As usual, a good first impression on this question can be obtained from the spontaneous case material. We find much the
same type of spontaneous experience widely scattered, not only
back through history to ancient times, but over widely distinct
ethnic groups as well. The Australian aborigines have spontaneous psi experiences quite similar to those of the American
population and the Western European. They are very similar to
the scattered examples reported from the peoples of modern China
or India or Japan, and those picked up from the American Indian
and the American Negro resemble in essential outlines those of
the white Americans. If the occurrence of these spontaneous psi
experiences is an indication, as it may properly be considered to
be in view of the laboratory verification of the capacity, then it is
fair to suggest that the psi function is widely enough distributed
to be considered a normal capacity of the species.

The experimental studies, too, have confirmed psi ability in
different ethnic, national, and sub-racial groupings, albeit only in
a very exploratory way. Among those who have been tested and
found to exhibit significant evidence of psi capacity, at least in
introductory tests, are Australian aborigines, American Indians,
American Negroes, Japanese, Indians, Spanish Americans, Western Europeans, and Americans.

Moreover, the study of various groups within a given culture
has left the impression that psi capacity is a general one with
no particular type or grouping of people showing *no* ability and
with none being exceptionally gifted. Various kinds of special
groups within the American or European culture have been
tested for ESP and they gave in most instances at least marginally
positive results; for example, there have been groups of mental
patients in the hospitals and of feeble-minded children in schools
for the subnormal. Tests have been made with a wide range of

people of different ages and, of course, both sexes. Groups of blind children have yielded results that compared with those of seeing children of the same age, and a few at least of the practitioners of the occult, such as mediums, astrologers, palmists, yogis, and dowsers, have been tried. While no group of any size has been found completely devoid of capacity to demonstrate ESP, at the same time no subdivision of the human species has been found to stand out in any really distinctive way as either possessing superior psi powers or superior control over them.

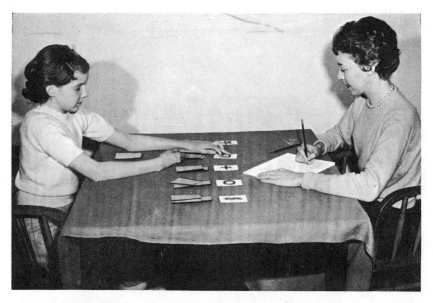

ESP test for the blind. The subject is trying to match sealed ESP cards to key cards with raised symbols.

Furthermore, among all the many attempts made in various cultures down through the ages to develop psi practices of one kind or another none has ever succeeded sufficiently to lead to any widespread practical use today. This indicates that as yet no class or group has been able to acquire a practical mastery over the ability either by reason of an exceptional inherited gift or through special cultivation of the normal endowment. The fact then that the ability *is* present in man is matched by the equally obvious fact that it can be expressed only to a limited degree.

But at the same time that psi is limited in the extent of its exercise in the individual, no evidence has thus far been found of any limitation within the species. The capacity is, therefore, a part of the normal equipment of the species.

E. Psi in Animals

The fact that psi was found to have so wide a distribution within the human species naturally raised the question as to where it originated in the evolutionary scheme. There was more to encourage this question, however, than the wide distribution of ESP capacity over the human race. For instance, a great many examples of unexplainable animal behavior were found that clearly suggested the possibility of an ESP function.[10] Suggestions to that effect have even been made by an occasional zoologist or naturalist confronted with this puzzling type of behavior. Among the more familiar animal feats that still stand unexplained in the textbooks of biology are remarkable instances of long migratory travel of certain species in the course of their annual movements from one part of the earth to another. It is not known as yet how certain species of birds are guided for hundreds and even thousands of miles over unbroken water—i.e., without landmarks. Similarly, marine animals cross the ocean or travel in some instances for hundreds of miles and in others even thousands in their migrations. In many species the mode of navigation in this long-distance orientation is entirely unknown. This does not, of course, mean that it is done by ESP; but it does mean that there is a possibility for the ESP hypothesis; in fact no other hypothesis has been presented yet that, as with ESP, has already been established as a genuine occurrence in nature.

More convincing to many students of these matters are the performances of domesticated animals in finding their way home over long distances, sometimes after having been taken away in closed vehicles by an indirect routine. Examples of animals traveling many hundreds of miles are reported and such reports involve many different species. Even more baffling still are the instances, fewer in number but numerous enough to be still impressive, in which a pet animal—dog, cat, or bird—left behind when its human companions departed for a new location, escaped later and followed them, arriving after some weeks or months at the new destination, sometimes hundreds of miles away and where it had never been before. These and other instances have opened up a new area of interest—the question of psi in animals.

Experimental work has been begun which has already produced evidence of good exploratory character that at least one horse,[11] a few dogs,[12] and a number of cats have shown behavior consistent only with the psi hypothesis.[13,14] The two experimental researches with cats by Osis and associates at Duke approach the conclusive level.

We can tentatively say, then, that not only is psi normal to the extent that it is very probably a natural function of the human individual regardless of health or intelligence or other classification, but that it is probably normal also to a great deal more of the animal world than our own species, although to just how much of it is not at this stage known.

II. The Place of Psi in Personality

A. How Psi Effects Are Manifested

Psi is a means of interaction between a person and his universe, a method of subject-object interaction. As already stated, its functioning parallels that of the sensorimotor system on which depends our familiar subject-object relations, the difference being that in the psi function the essential operation is known to be nonphysical. This is true in spite of the fact that in order to be objectively manifested psi must be converted into an observable physical effect. In its psychokinetic action it can be registered only as an influence upon a physical system. Similarly, on the cognitive side, in extrasensory perception the information acquired must be converted into the conscious experience of the individual, either as an hallucination, a dream, or an intuitive way of knowing about an objective situation, or as some indirectly grasped expression or manifestation conveying the message (e.g., motor automatisms, compulsions, etc.).

Furthermore, there are no known specific receptors for ESP impressions, and no known motor organs or functions directly involved in PK. Whatever psi represents, no differentiation within the organism has been discovered such as has evolved in the form of the sensorimotor system. Psi appears to be more elemental, more primitive—at any rate more unspecialized.

B. No Organic Localization Known

Trying as we are in present research in parapsychology to bring psi processes into their place in natural science, it should be remembered that this natural science lies within a framework given us by the senses themselves. That means we are attempting to describe psi functions in the terms of and in connection with a universe that itself has been pictured only in sensorially descriptive concepts. This naturally tends to represent the phenomena of psi in terms of contrasts rather than by positive characteristics. But at this stage clear differentiation is of primary importance. We must, accordingly, begin with the fact that psi is not only nonphysical; it does not have as yet any discovered organic (e.g., cerebral) localization, and it is not directly observable. It is encountered only in the form of a converted effect.

C. But Psi Is Voluntary

On the positive side, however, is the unmistakable characteristic that psi is, within limits, subject to the volitional or purposive control of the individual. The subject gives a degree of specific conscious orientation to the function. Otherwise to carry out the types of test in use would be impossible, for in these a given target at a specified time and place is usually in conscious focus. Even the spontaneous cases themselves, though experienced by the individual without conscious effort (otherwise they would not be spontaneous) are still recognizedly purposive in quality. The urges and interests of the individual are, as a rule, obviously deeply involved. In the test situation the persons participating can carry out the instructions given them of attempting to identify a given card in a given location and even at a specified time. This dirigibility of psi is extremely important in identifying it as a normal function of the personality. In spite of the seemingly profound difference between psi and the sensorimotor functions, this one feature of being to a certain extent a voluntary function would alone serve to tie in psi capacity firmly as a basic aspect of personality.

D. It Is Unconscious

Let us turn back now to another characteristic, perhaps the principal distinction of psi in addition to its extraphysical nature. The long-unsuspected fact is that the essential psi function is an unconscious one. It is now recognized that while psi phenomena are known to occur for the most part only with conscious individuals as subjects (including dreaming, trance, etc. as states of restricted consciousness), the basic process itself is unconscious. Unlike sensory perception, in ESP the individual in his conscious recognition of the phenomena gets only a converted aftereffect or secondary result. In the successful test demonstration, the fact that the function has operated seems to elude his conscious focus.

Among spontaneous cases a wide variety of types of effects resulting from ESP's operation has been reported. As L. E. Rhine[15] has classified these types she finds them largely assignable to four main categories: First, there are intuitive experiences in which the subject just knows in an unaccountable way of some event he could not have perceived sensorially or known from memory, reasoning, or lucky guess. Second, he may experience a veridical or meaningful hallucination; that is, the truth conveyed to him is projected in such a way that he sees, hears, smells, or "feels" the essential message, much as if the actual occurrence were present to his senses. Third, he may, in some symbolic way, dramatize the message in a dream (or daydream) experience so that he has to interpret it to get at the meaning conveyed. Fourth, he may dream (or daydream) the scene itself in all literal detail, experiencing a pictorial realization of a meaningful event.

All four of these mechanisms are only ways of translating the underlying psi function into meaningful information. The awareness of psi itself remains unconscious, and therefore obscure, even though there is often in the subject's consciousness a definite conviction or sense of the importance, the reality, or the compelling urgency of the meaning of the experience. This feeling of conviction, too, appears to be a secondary or translated effect. It is a judgment that derives from the subject's interpretation of the experience; it is converted to consciousness as an aftereffect; the determining function still remains hidden.

The same is borne out, though less vividly, of course, in the experimental studies themselves.[16] Even the subjects who have succeeded most consistently and strikingly could not reliably tell the experimenter how they were able to succeed so well, though sometimes explanations were offered. Nor were they able to tell reliably when they were most successful. Reports of introspective observation which the subject himself takes seriously have yielded nothing useful and convincing to the experimenter. In several experiments subjects have attempted to indicate which of their ESP calls are correct, but little or no indication has been found that they can recognize the difference between the use of psi and mere guessing. Even if future work along these lines should discover a way by which subjects would be able to make the distinction, it would not necessarily show that psi had become conscious; the possibility would remain that the distinction was made by means of ESP or by the identification of some secondary effect attending the psi operation.

The fact that psi functions in an unconscious way ties in interestingly enough with the fact that it is nonphysical and that it may well have originated far back in the evolution of the living world. All this suggests that consciousness itself is a derivation of the evolution of sensory experience through the interaction of the individual with the specialized physical stimuli of the environment. Moreover, the more elementary and possibly primordial psi function which has to manifest itself through secondary sensory-physical operations may antedate these sensory functions and thus may constitute a more fundamental aspect of the organism than do consciousness and sensory experiences. These are at this stage tentative lines of thought suggested by the facts.

E. Unusual Effects of the Unconsciousness of Psi

The fact that psi is unconscious will explain many odd things about it. Some of these curious effects are among the most interesting features in the data of parapsychology. Some of them, too, have added a great deal to the proof value of the evidence. Some have almost come to be considered as earmarks of psi, so that the investigator may rightly treat them as valid evidence; for example, the significant decline in scoring rate within the test unit (the run, column, set, page, etc.) or the tendency of the subject to score reliably *below* the chance average under certain conditions, or the consistent way in which some subjects *miss* a specified symbol by calling it, more often than chance would average, by some other symbol name, or their occasional tendency to *displace* and hit the target next to the one intended and to hold consistently to this oblique way of responding.

These are all well-established by-products of psi investigations that have been encountered by many research workers. They are not typical of conscious, sensory perception, and they are at least partly the result of the fact that the subject cannot profit from his success and failure. The psi process does not give the basis for learning by which introspection can associate error with the awareness of what was done wrong. In a word, learning in the specific sense in which the word is used in psychology should not be expected under the conditions in which psi operates.

As one can readily see, this unconsciousness of psi has made its investigation extremely difficult. It would help to explain why the many efforts to train subjects to better performance have not been successful. Not even the effort on the part of the subject to learn by testing himself and by making an immediate checkup on his success and failure has led to any remarkable improvement.* This indicates that something more is lacking than knowledge of success and failure as such. An essential part of the learning function would presumably involve an awareness of the method by which the right or wrong response had been made. At this point one can only ask whether there may be an insurmountable barrier here to the improvement of psi performance through learning. But this is another frontier awaiting study.

F. Psi-missing

The unconsciousness of psi has created much havoc in the

---

* The outstanding example of a long series of tests with the subject knowing immediately of success or failure after each trial is the work of G. N. M. Tyrrell; yet his subject did not show any improvement of scores with practice under these conditions (see Smith[17]).

LIBRARY ST. MARY'S COLLEGE

research field because of an effect that has come to be called *psi-missing*.[18] This is a merely descriptive term covering the tendency of some subjects under certain conditions to give significantly negative deviations; that is, to average below mean chance expectation. Such negative scoring is due to the fact that any condition which systematically disturbs psi in such test conditions as are now standard (allowing deviation above or below the theoretical mean and requiring a response to a regular given number of possibilities) is bound to produce a reversal of deviation. Anything the subject may inadvertently do to depart systematically from the correct way of exercising psi (for him) would count against even his scoring at chance level. If, for example, he normally scores highest by taking the first symbol that comes to mind, then when he cautiously decides to make a practice of waiting instead for a later, more vivid one, he will be sure to induce psi-missing. It would not matter for what reason the subject changed his practice, whether unconscious negativism or just a curious urge to try a different device. The result would be the same—an unwitting rejection of the target.

It is a good question whether psi is the only function that suffers from this odd reversal effect. It seems very probable that the frustrating consequences of this type of systematic error of judgment operating on an unconscious level might have wide bearings for general psychology, more especially for its abnormal problem areas. Thus far, however, it looks like a new effect—one unknown to the general field. It has, indeed, created disruptively abnormal effects for the parapsychologist; as, for example, when a subject in participating in long runs of trials develops at the mid-point or thereabouts (as some have done) a sort of cumulative strain that induces a psi-missing tendency for the rest of the run. The score total will be dismissed as a chance result, yet there may well be a highly significant decline distribution within the run.

G. Psi-missing and Partial Perception

On the positive side of the ledger of psi values there is something to be credited to the unconsciousness of psi and especially to its most outstanding consequence, psi-missing. One of the more illuminating points the evidence for psi-missing has brought out is that psi is not an all-or-none function. For example, when a subject responds to an ESP card in a test the indications are that he does not either completely know or not know which it is in the absolute degree that usually applies let us say to uninhibited visual perception. This is brought out by the fact that in a number of experiments in which the ability to score below chance was compared with the capacity for scoring above, the deviations were numerically similar. Yet it can be seen that if a subject knew for certain, let us say, 20 cards out of 100, and could only get "chance" (20 per cent) on the rest, he could expect 36 per cent as the most likely score in the normal test, i.e., a positive deviation of 16 per cent. If, however, he were deliberately or unconsciously *trying to score low* and still knew 20 of the 100 cards, he should expect to get 16 correct by chance, a negative deviation of 4 per cent.

The fact mentioned above, that in actual tests in which psi-missing occurs approximately as large a deviation (negative, of course) may be produced as normally is produced by psi-hitting, indicates that less knowledge is needed to say what a card is *not* than to say what it is. To equal in a negative (psi-missing) series the positive score of 36 per cent would require a score of only 4 per cent or a negative deviation of 16 per cent. To get this would require a little knowledge about a lot more cards than the 20 assumed in the illustration above. This indicates that perception in ESP, as in the marginal zone of sensory perception, is *partial*, not absolute. And in many respects it appears to be processed through the same type of judgmental exchange as occurs in marginally conscious or subconscious sensory functions. This and other useful clues are mainly by-products of the psi-missing studies.

H. Some Mental States Associated with Psi-missing

Psi-missing has also enabled investigators to give some intelligent interpretation to a large array of curiously conflicting results obtained from a wide range of different investigations. Most common in this array are the tests dealing with personality correlates of ESP test performance; that is, the study of measures of personality that seem to be related to scoring level in ESP. For example, the studies of Schmeidler[19] at City College, New York, brought out the fact that if students tested in the classroom for ESP capacity were first separated on the basis of their attitude toward the possibility of ESP, the results showed a different level of scoring for those who were favorable (sheep) and for those who were skeptical (goats). The sheep as a group almost invariably averaged higher than the goats. The goats, however, scored below mean

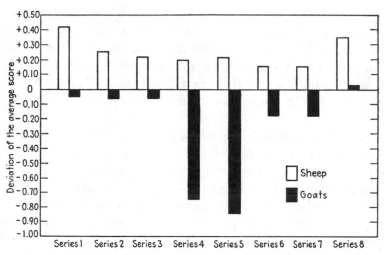

Effect of attitude upon ESP test performance. The sheep are those subjects who accept or are open-minded to the possibility of ESP, while the goats reject it (Schmeidler).

chance expectation and did so with a degree of consistency that was impressive. The difference between the sheep and goats has over the years of testing contributed a phenomenally significant difference between the amassed data of the two groups.

Now it was quite evident in this work that the principle of separation was concerned more with the sign (or direction) of the deviation of the scoring of a given subject than with the amount of ESP measured. The attitude of the subjects allowed a separation of the individuals in the classes on the one hand into one group that tended to score positively and a second group on the other hand that preponderantly scored a negative deviation. The fact is, the goats showed statistical evidence of an ESP effect just as the sheep did.

This repeated result is typical of a fairly large number of investigations; some of these involved the registration of the attitude of the subject toward the test,[20] others recorded certain mental states (or physiological accompaniments) occurring during the test.[21] Some were aimed at estimating a general trait such as extraversion-introversion,[22] still others dealt with patterns of interest,[23] and there were still other psychological estimates tried.[24] In all this we are dealing with essentially exploratory work, although some of it was done under conditions approximating the verification level. A number of these measures have proved effective to a degree in separating high scorers from low. And not only that, they have thrown the group representing one end of the scale of personality measurement as far below the chance mean as the other end of the scale placed the other group above. This indicates that what was being measured was not a mental state correlated with the ESP process but, rather, an aspect of test performance—a part having to do with the psi-missing effect; that is, the correlated mental state did not determine how much ESP would function but whether it would produce a negative or a positive deviation, whether it would consistently hit or consistently miss the target. Thus far, then, certainly most of the measurements made on correlated personality or general mental states have had to do with that specific (psi-missing) element in the sensitive mechanism of psi-in-the-test-situation. When the more favorable conditions prevailed, the subject was able to get positive results. At the other end of the scale the same amount of ESP operated but it was twisted somehow in expression and resulted as an avoidance of the target. This is indeed one of the interesting puzzles for future study.

III. Conditions Affecting Psi

The exercise of psi capacity is more difficult to control or command than that of most other known mental processes, but, as we have already seen, this matter of control is relative. Psi is subject to some voluntary control even though its essential functioning is unconscious; that is, it is subject to volitional direction as to the objective, the target selected, the timing, and other specified features. It appears, then, that psi is a dirigible or controllable faculty of personality even though at present the limitations of control are so great as to allow little use or application of the ability.

A. The Role of Motivation

Now the most important controlling factor in mental life in general is drive or motivation. All of the abilities of men and animals are naturally dependent upon this striving or motivational influence. It appears to be no less the case with psi. In fact, one of the impressions gained from the study of spontaneous cases is that in most of them the conative nature of the experience is obvious[25] and usually a strong purpose is involved. Often a powerful urge is evident behind the experience, perhaps the need of one of a pair of deeply-attached individuals to reach the other in a crisis, the need to know of an impending event threatening a loved one. These are familiar types, although less strongly motivated ones are also common.

Such motivation as just mentioned cannot, of course, be introduced into the standard tests, desirable as such a method would be from the point of view of providing conditions for maximum scoring. But experimental evidence, too, indicates that the subject's motivation is important. The grounds provided by certain special researches are rather good for attributing value in raising ESP scores to the use of rewards or prizes adapted to the subject's age and interest.[26] But even in the average psi experiment there is (or should be) lively interest and drive. In the average normal individual there may be a desire to impress the experimenter or to stand out well among the other subjects. He may even be driven by scientific enthusiasm, or, again, by his own individual curiosity concerning his abilities. Obviously the extent to which these motivating states can be developed depends greatly upon the individual himself, the type of test situation, and the experimenter in charge.

The striking results of ESP tests often obtained with strongly motivated subjects indicate better than anything else the importance of the factor of interest. Instances are on record in which subjects produced extremely high scores during intervals of intense interest and enthusiasm. The indications of the high-pitched drive involved are reasonably good. In one example of a perfect score of twenty-five the subject at the end remarked, "You will never get me to do that again!" In another, following a score of twenty-two hits out of twenty-five trials, the 10-year old boy who was the subject became nauseated from the excitement developed by the experimenter's encouragement throughout the series of several runs culminating in the high score. In the series of tests conducted by Riess[27] in which a perfect score of twenty-five was obtained toward the end and the over-all average was above eighteen out of twenty-five, the test was interrupted by the illness of the subject, diagnosed as hyperthyroidism. It was reported that the family of the subject considered that the experiments were a factor, a source of nervous strain, suggesting that she was highly motivated. These and other outstanding performances accompanied by evidences of extreme effort on the part of the participant have led investigators to attach the greatest importance to having the subject, whenever possible, approach the test with a driving interest.

At the other extreme, where scoring rate in psi tests approaches a pure chance average, as it does in a great deal of experimental work, the factor most likely responsible is again the subject's motivation. It should be emphasized, especially for those contemplating an actual test program involving psi capacity, that a merely casual interest in taking a test (let us say, at the request of a teacher or friend) is not enough to enable the average individual to produce evidence of psi. This is probably the reason why many of those exploratory experimenters who from time to time undertake to conduct an ESP test series with a class or lecture audience obtain only an insignificant result. (It is true there may be a degree of psi activity involved that can easily be over-looked because the results of the subjects who score positively by ESP may be canceled out by others who show psi-missing. Such slight effects can only be discovered by a systematic analysis of the data on a prearranged plan, such as Schmeidler's sheep-goat distinction.)

The fact that needs emphasis in psi research today, however, is that such low-level scoring in mass tests, even when it is acceptably significant, is far below the potential of the individual subjects involved—i.e., below the level of performance of which many of them are capable when strongly activated to achieve their utmost. It is, in fact, necessary for almost everyone to be keenly inspired to exercise his psi-ability to a marked degree. Rare individuals can, it is true, do well while appearing to play at the tests with a seemingly indifferent manner—though this appearance may not give the true picture of the effort involved. Certainly some subjects can perform well—for a time at least—with less effort than the average person would require. Most people, however, need to be led up to participation in the test in such a way as to feel its challenge to the full, and to be moved to exert their utmost in an intelligent and concentrated manner, free of doubts and other distractions and uncomplicated by rational inhibitions.

All this is obviously a very difficult state of mind to induce, either in one's self or in others. Sometimes it can be brought about or incidentally caught momentarily but under conditions that do not long continue. The use of hypnosis in creating such a state of mind at once suggests itself, but it has not been established as yet that the state induced by that means is more than a simulation of the desired effect. The lack of control over psi attainable by hypnosis may be due to the lack of complete acceptance of the suggestion on a level that genuinely affects psi functioning. On the other hand, the good results obtained in group tests of ESP with children would seem to be due to the transparent candor of the age level in revealing its attitudes, thus giving the experimenter a clear index of motivation—and thus enabling him to work up the required enthusiasm before testing. The children have not yet acquired the manners and habits that cover up their spontaneous attitudes.

B. The Complications of Psi-missing

The driving interest or enthusiasm of the subject for the achievement of high scores does not, however, determine whether the subject will score positively or negatively (i.e., *above* or *below* the chance average). Two different sets of factors are involved, one determining the amount of psi and the other, the sign (positive or negative) of its deviation. The test conditions may be such as to induce a psi-missing effect. In such a case the more the subject is motivated the larger the negative deviation will be. This has been brought out under comparative experimental tests by the use of rewards. These experiments imply that the subject's drive has much to do with the *amount* of evidence of ESP (size of deviation) he will give, but that quite a different set of factors have to do with whether the result will be one of hitting or of missing (which sign the deviation will have). Obviously it is very important to realize that these two independent factors are to be dealt with, for both affect the results.

While the strength of motivation of the subject is the primary consideration influencing the amount of evidence of psi he can produce, there are many conditions that can affect the sign of deviation. As we have already indicated, there are many states of mind which, in the subject, can upset psi-hitting and convert it into psi-missing. In experiments the worst aspect of this complication has been that psi-missing often comes in to dilute or cancel the positive deviation contributed either by other subjects or by the same subjects at an earlier stage. The swing over to the negative side of chance expectation is not always discovered in time or in such a way that its cancelling effect can be avoided. It may come about as a decline of scoring rate in the run or set or record page or other unit of the total data. One grouping of subjects may give negative effects while the others give positive; or, if the experiment is a complicated one with more than one type of test or condition, one condition may give a negative deviation and the other a positive one. More often than not when a variety of conditions are involved the subjects have a preference and the condition least liked produces psi-missing. It is, therefore, extremely important for the experimenter to consider these possible unstabilizing influences in the design of his experiments, in his selection of subjects, and in the exploratory or pilot-testing stage.[28]

It is known that in general in a typical group of subjects those who are more introverted, more skeptically inclined, and least satisfied with the testing personnel are more likely to get negative deviations. On the other hand, those who are more favorably oriented, more extraverted, more self-confident and generally enthusiastic are most likely to average on the positive side. Conditions that put the subject under strain, impress him with the difficulty or absurdity of the task, and develop intellectual conflict or tension are reasonably certain to lower the scoring rate below the mean expected from chance. Or if a comparison of conditions is involved in the test, the unavoidable development of a preference on the part of a subject is likely to play a part in the delicate mechanism which decides whether the subject will hit or miss the target. Observations like these are, in great part, well-established although some are only the working impressions of experienced investigators. It would be safe enough to take either category rather seriously in planning or interpreting research.

Perhaps the best way to summarize the facts known about the effect of psychological conditions in psi testing is to formulate recommendations to psi investigators, and Chapter 7 will serve that purpose.

References

1. RHINE, J. B.: Psi phenomena and psychiatry. *Proc. Roy. Soc. Med.*, *43*:804–814, 1950.
2. RHINE, J. B.: Extrasensory perception and hypnosis, in *Experimental Hypnosis*, L. M. LeCron, editor. New York, Macmillan, 1952, pp. 359–368.
3. SHULMAN, R.: A study of card-guessing in psychotic subjects. *J. Parapsychol.*, *2*:95–106, 1938.
4. BATES, K. E., and NEWTON, M.: An experimental study of ESP capacity in mental patients. *J. Parapsychol.*, *15*:271–277, 1951.
5. SCHMEIDLER, G. R.: ESP performance and the Rorschach test: A survey of recent experiments. *J. Soc. Psychical Res.*, *35*:323–339, 1950.
6. SMITH, B. M., and HUMPHREY, B. M.: Some personality characteristics related to ESP performance. *J. Parapsychol.*, *10*:269–289, 1946.
7. NICOL, J. F., and HUMPHREY, B. M.: The exploration of ESP and human personality. *J. Am. Soc. Psychical Res.*, *47*:133–178, 1953.
8. BOND, E. M.: General extrasensory perception with a group of fourth and fifth grade retarded children. *J. Parapsychol.*, *1*:114–122, 1937.

9. HUMPHREY, B. M.:   ESP and intelligence.   *J. Parapsychol.,* 9:7–16, 1945.

10. RHINE, J. B.:   The present outlook on the question of psi in animals. *J. Parapsychol., 15*:230–251, 1951.

11. RHINE, J. B., and RHINE, L. E.:   An investigation of a "mind-reading" horse.   *J. Abnorm. & Social Psychol., 23*:449–466, 1929.

12. BECHTEREV, V.:   "Direct influence" of a person upon the behavior of animals.   *J. Parapsychol., 13*:166–176, 1949 (translated and condensed from *Ztschr. Psychotherapie,* 1924).

13. OSIS, K.:   A test of the occurrence of a psi effect between man and the cat.   *J. Parapsychol., 16*:233–256, 1952.

14. OSIS, K., and FOSTER, E. B.:   A test of ESP in cats.   *J. Parapsychol., 17*:168–186, 1953.

15. RHINE, L. E.:   Subjective forms of spontaneous psi experiences.   *J. Parapsychol., 17*:77–114, 1953.

16. RHINE, J. B.:   The source of the difficulties in parapsychology.   *J. Parapsychol., 10*:162–168, 1946.

17. SMITH, B. M.:   The Tyrrell experiments.   *J. Parapsychol., 1*:63–69, 1937.

18. RHINE, J. B.:   The problem of psi-missing.   *J. Parapsychol., 16*:90–129, 1952.

19. SCHMEIDLER, G. R., and MURPHY, G.:   The influence of belief and disbelief in ESP upon individual scoring levels.   *J. Exper. Psychol., 36*:271–276, 1946.

20. WOODRUFF, J. L., and DALE, L. A.:   Subject and experimenter attitudes in relation to ESP scoring.   *J. Am. Soc. Psychical Res., 44*:87–112, 1950.

21. BRUGMANS, H. J. F. W.:   Some experiments in telepathy performed in the Psychological Institute of the University of Gröningen. *Compte-Rendu du Premier Congrès International des Recherches Psychiques,* 1921.

22. HUMPHREY, B. M.:   Introversion-extroversion ratings in relation to scores in ESP tests.   *J. Parapsychol., 15*:252–262, 1951.

23. STUART, C. E.:   An interest inventory relation to ESP scores.   *J. Parapsychol., 10*:154–161, 1946.

24. HUMPHREY, B. M.:   Success in ESP as related to form of response drawings: I. Clairvoyance experiments.   *J. Parapsychol., 10*: 78–106, 1946; II. GESP experiments.   *J. Parapsychol., 10*:181–196, 1946.

25. MURPHY, G.:   Psychical phenomena and human needs.   *J. Am. Soc. Psychical Res., 37*:163–191, 1943.

26. RHINE, J. B.: Experiments bearing upon the precognition hypothesis: II. Mechanically selected cards. *J. Parapsychol.*, 5:1–57, 1941 (see also pp. 36–38).
27. RIESS, B. F.: A case of high scores in card guessing at a distance. *J. Parapsychol.*, 1:260–263, 1937.
28. RHINE, J. B.: Conditions favoring success in psi tests. *J. Parapsychol.*, 12:58–75, 1948.

Additional Reading

FOSTER, A. A.: ESP tests with American Indian children. *J. Parapsychol.*, 7:94–103, 1943.
FOSTER, A. A.: Is ESP diametric? *J. Parapsychol.*, 4:325–328, 1940.
HUMPHREY, B. M.: ESP score level predicted by a combination of measures of personality. *J. Parapsychol.*, 14:193–206, 1950.
HUMPHREY, B. M.: ESP tests with mental patients before and after electroshock treatment. *J. Soc. Psychical Res.*, 37:259–266, 1954.
HUMPHREY, B. M.: Paranormal occurrences among preliterate peoples. *J. Parapsychol.*, 8:214–229, 1944.
HUMPHREY, B. M., and NICOL, J. F.: The exploration of ESP and human personality. *J. Am. Soc. Psychical. Res.*, 47:133–178, 1953.
MURPHY, G.: Personality appraisal and the paranormal. *J. Am. Soc. Psychical. Res.*, 41:3–11, 1947.
NICOL, J. F., and HUMPHREY, B. M.: The repeatability problem in ESP-personality research. *J. Am. Soc. Psychical. Res.*, 49:125–156, 1955.
PRATT, J. G.: The homing problem in pigeons. *J. Parapsychol.*, 17:34–60, 1953.
RHINE, L. E.: *Hidden Channels of the Mind.* New York, Sloane, 1961.
ROSE, R.: *Living Magic.* New York, Rand McNally, 1956.
ROSE, R.: Experiments in ESP and PK with aboriginal subjects. *J. Parapsychol.*, 16:219–220, 1952.
THOULESS, R. H., and WIESNER, B. P.: On the nature of psi phenomena. *J. Parapsychol.*, 10:107–119, 1946.
THOULESS, R. H., and WIESNER, B. P: The psi processes in normal and 'paranormal" psychology. *J. Parapsychol.*, 12:192–212, 1948.

Chapter 6

Psi Research and Other Related Fields

SINCE this is not a book of interpretation, we do not attempt to go into even the most obvious of the far-reaching implications and bearings of the findings of parapsychology. Although a good case can be made for the view that interpretation is an integral part of a science, it does not follow that the entire picture has always to appear between the same covers. But even while confining ourselves, as committed, to a strictly factual emphasis, there remains the task of reviewing the common research frontiers that have opened up between parapsychology and the adjacent disciplines or problem areas closely enough related to have overlapping interests.

This further review can be seen as a continuation of the two immediately preceding chapters. In them the facts of psi relating to physics were first presented and then the findings relating to general psychology. Now we shall go on to other fields with which psi is less deeply involved than with the two mentioned. Some of the adjoining areas are branches of science while others are fields of practice or professional work. In this survey the aim will be to follow the frontier of the application of psi itself rather than any systematic plan of curricular division.

1. Psi in Practice

Little actual practice survives today that is identified, at least by the practitioners themselves, with psi capacity. As scientific thinking extended its influence over modern cultures, practices that depended upon so "unscientific" a theory as psi seemed to be naturally looked upon with disapproval. This would follow, whatever their merits, especially if, as we should expect with psi, there were also considerable difficulty in the practical application of the capacity.

However, it is not easy to be sure whether or not success in such practices is due to psi or to some other ability or function. To begin with, most practices today that might involve psi are believed by the practitioners to depend upon some other principle or rationale, and even such beliefs may vary from one community, from one individual, to another. For example, in such practices as palmistry and astrology theories and systems of practical guidance are laid down which in operation allow considerable latitude for the practitioner's interpretative judgment and intuitive impression. Such interpretation could well depend on psi. We cite these, however, to illustrate areas of investigation that have not produced results that merit scientific acceptance.

Two areas of practice of this general type, however, have been brought far enough into scientific perspective, at least in an exploratory way, to have won a certain amount of scientific interest. The more important and conspicuous of these is the practice of *mediumship.* In this case the theory of the believers in the practice is that discarnate spirits communicate with the living by using the practitioner as a medium or instrument. But since this theory itself would, if valid, have a religious importance much greater than any of the merely practical consequences, we shall leave the discussion of it as a research project to the section on psi and religion.

The other practice is what is known as *dowsing* or, as it has been commonly practiced, the divination for underground water or minerals. Dowsing is a combination, on the one hand, of a motor automatism or unconscious muscular movement and, on the other, of some sort of extrasensory guidance to discovery of the location of a specified object or substance. In the most familiar type of the practice the dowser is asked to find a suitable location for a well; he takes a forked twig by the two small ends and, holding it in such a way that it tends to swing easily and with very delicate pressure, he walks over the ground until the rod swings downward. Generally the dowser believes he is exerting no influence himself on the twig and that it is responding to forces emanating from the underground material he is seeking. There are many adaptations, modifications, and other variations of this procedure, the most common being the substitution of a pendulum for the twig. The pendulum method is more common in French speaking countries, and the name "radiesthesia" has been associated with the practice with the pendulum as compared with "dowsing" applied to the movement of the rod or twig. The pendulum is more convenient to use over maps and the practice has been adapted to use a diagram or map of the terrain where the location of the water (or other substance) is desired.

In recent years in the U. S. A. a more sophisticated and urbanized form of dowsing has been developed, mainly by practical workers in public utility organizations. These people, confronted with the problem of locating underground pipes and other structures, have developed the practice of using as dowsing "instruments" metal rods with right angles, one in each hand, held in such a way that they swing very easily as the "locator" walks over the area to be explored. The belief of those who use them is that the rods will swing when they cross over the pipe. The practice is also widespread in and around the petroleum industry. There have been numerous modifications of this dowsing or "doodle-bug" type of exploration.

In spite of the widespread and still active practice of dowsing comparatively little research has been carried out on the problem it presents. One reason for this is that it is very difficult, if not impossible, to make a dependable evaluation of reports of practical results, even when they are available. It is sometimes possible to check up on the success of individual dowsers, but usually impossible to determine how much knowledge from more familiar sources the individual dowser may have had. Chance cannot be estimated, either, and control tests are not very efficient.

Yet researches have been undertaken. The efforts that have been made thus far have nearly all taken the direction of first modifying the practice itself sufficiently to allow the introduction of at least preliminary control. For example, dowsers reputed to be successful in locating underground water have been tried on underground pipes in which the water is known to be flowing. In the preliminary tests that were made the rod turned as the dowser passed over the ground where the pipe was buried. But when he was then told the water had been turned off, and when he again passed over the pipe location, the rod did not turn. Then he was ready for a test in which the action of the rod, as the dowser walked back and forth over the ground in which the pipe was laid, should be taken as an indicator as to how well the dowser could tell when he was over running water. With this technique and a cooperative dowser and with attention to the psychological need of the dowser to keep up his confidence in the rod, possibilities were found for a little exploratory research on the problem.

Under such conditions sufficiently encouraging results have been obtained to justify the continuance of the study.[1-3] As a matter of fact, results have been comparable to those of ESP card tests with beginning subjects. They lend weight to the view which most workers in parapsychology would take, that dowsing, if and when it is really successful under conditions in which rational judgment could not explain the results, is a combination of unconscious muscular movement and clairvoyant ESP. Several points of similarity between the test data of dowsing and ESP support this interpretation.

Some of the exploratory experiments in dowsing have been carried out using hidden coins or other objects considered by the dowser as acceptable targets.[4] The rate of success in these tests was of the order of scoring obtained in the more familiar types of ESP tests. There is, however, nothing thus far to indicate that the use of the motor automatism is in itself of any value to the ESP testing procedure. It has a secondary virtue, however, in that for some subjects it encourages stronger belief in their ability; such a belief helps to generate and sustain interest in the test. In this the seeming independence of the automatic movement may be a supporting factor, since it makes it appear impersonal.

The example of dowsing represents a wide front of possible application of psi to the affairs of real life. As understanding of the psi function develops and control over its operation increases we shall hear more about applications; but we must expect the development to be slow and gradual on account of the depth at which the function is embedded in the unconscious mental system of the individual.

II. Psi in Psychiatry

This section takes us far away from the kind of practice involved in mediumship and dowsing, yet it leaves us still within the wide scope of practical problems, in this instance strictly personal or human ones. As we indicated in the preceding chapter, a fair amount of exploratory investigation has been carried out in mental hospitals, using the mentally ill as subjects in tests for ESP. These introductory inquiries were made either to see whether subjects in certain psychopathological states might be discovered that would give more outstanding results in ESP tests than the general average of normal subjects or to see if any connection could be found between mental illness and parapsychical abilities. In recalling these studies in the present somewhat different connection, it is well to remember that they have been comparatively few, as well as considerably scattered, efforts. No one of the researches made, and not even all together, could properly be considered as constituting a thoroughly exhaustive study of all the possible associations of psi and mental disorder to the degree the question merits.

Perhaps the greatest reason for cautious judgment at this point lies in the fact that in all the studies the effort consisted in carrying into the mental hospitals tests devised for the laboratory and for normal volunteer subjects.[5-8] There is then some psychological basis for supposing that the tests may not be properly and fairly comparative. A test designed for a well man may not always be a comparably effective test for a sick man, and vice versa. When we recall that psi is the most mercurial of all mental phenomena yet studied, we can appreciate the need for caution in looking at the results of these mental hospital tests of ESP.

The great need for the investigation of psi in mental patients is for a proper clinical test or, rather, a testing system that would have within itself the necessary devices of adjustment to fit it to the various states and stages to which, if it is to be useful, it must easily be adapted. Since situations vary so extremely in the patient's world, special psychological requirements should be worked out for testing psi at the bedside. Such special standardizations and establishments of norms needed for clinical use must, of course, await the recognition of need by members of the professions concerned.

Not all of the researches on psi in the psychiatric area have been experimental. The case study methods that are themselves more conspicuous in this area have given rise to a considerable body of literature.[9] This group of studies has mainly to do with the occurrence of telepathy, usually between patient and psychiatrist in the course of psychiatric treatment. As the suggested readings on this topic listed in the section and at the end of the chapter will show, a number of articles, along with even a small number of books, give to this area of overlap between psi and psychiatry something of the appearance of a distinct branch or school. The degree to which the clinical study of telepathy in psychiatric practice has been fruitful is still a matter of individual judgment. The study has been mainly associated with psychoanalytic methods of therapy. The suggestive findings have not as yet been brought to the verification stage as they have to be before the results can be judged.

In one respect the psychiatrist is in an excellent position to deal intelligently with the psi function, especially if his patient shows spontaneous manifestations of psi or if psi can be induced experimentally. Probably no one else could have a comparable understanding of the personality of the individual to that which the psychiatrist could and should have before his professional treatment is completed. With this advantage he should be especially well situated to make discoveries regarding the functioning of psi in the mental life of the individual.

Another important common boundary is shared by the parapsychologist and the psychiatrist in their study of the personality of man. It is a conspicuous fact, one we suspect not very fully appreciated in parapsychology itself as yet, that psychiatry and parapsychology really deal with the same types of spontaneous surface phenomena. No other two fields, for example, have so great an appreciation of dreams. No other branch of study but psychiatry shares with parapsychology its recognition of the importance of such exceptional experiences as hallucinations, automatisms, odd intuitions, and compulsive motor responses. No other study of human nature shares with the psi investigator the interest in dream symbolism, dramatization, and distortion that psychiatry rather generally does.

And, of course, above all, the two branches are concerned with the more submerged area of personality, the unconscious level of mental life. When more pieces of the puzzle of man's nature have been fitted together and the pattern of unconscious mental functioning becomes clearer, there will likely be other common ground discovered; we suggest that the psi-missing effect that is so conspicuous a part of parapsychological study may be found to have its comparable effects in abnormal mental life. It may be responsible for some of those persistently perverse judgments which, systematically made with the best of conscious intention, contribute eventually to the ultimate derangement of the individual's life. They may be due to the same subconcious tendency which contributes a significant negative deviation in psi experiments. It is but one of many problems of magnitude that await the research worker along this frontier on the domain of mental disorder.

III. The Place of Psi in Education

Only in recent years has there been any effort made to bring the study of psi into the field of education. From time to time an occasional experiment in ESP had been carried out in a schoolroom, but these investigations were made largely in the interest of finding conveniently located subjects who were willing to participate in the tests. Likewise, investigations had been made of children in schools for the blind, in orphanages, and in institutions for mentally retarded children; but in none of these was the primary objective that of finding out what possible role psi might play in the educational operation itself, the exchange between teacher and pupil.

The first step in this area of investigation was taken in Holland, in the work of van Busschbach, himself an inspector of schools, in Amsterdam.[10] The point of view was distinctly that of the educator and the study was designed to discover whether, in the teacher-pupil relation, a psi factor might be an important element. The first step was to find out if psi could be demonstrated between teacher and pupils in the classroom situation. Resulting tests showed that the teacher, and only the teacher belonging to the particular classroom, did serve as a successful agent in tests of GESP. When substitute teachers or when pupils were agents instead of the regular teachers, the results obtained were attributable to chance. The repetition of the experiment by assistants in a second city of Holland[11] and in two American cities[12] showed that the finding had a much more general significance.

At the same time the delicate character of the psi function was well demonstrated too. Van Busschbach designed his test for the fifth and sixth grades and couched the instructions and psychological cast of the test in the language calculated to appeal to fifth and sixth graders; then, when he applied the test to seventh and eighth grade pupils and to still higher grades, he obtained only chance results. Likewise, comparable tests on still younger children were insignificant. These findings at this stage are of more evident significance to parapsychology than to education. Their importance lies mainly in the fact that they reveal a relationship already established—and a widely extended one—into which the ESP tests can be readily fitted. It looks as though a natural test situation has been found that is suited to the operation of psi.

On the side of education, however, the small beginning made has a greater importance than may at first appear. The results indicate that some communication on extrasensory lines is possible when the teacher and pupils are in a certain state of established relations. This is the beginning, necessarily slender and tenuous, for a line of research that might reveal much of what is still unknown about conditions essential to the best teacher-pupil exchange. A more recent study from the Duke Laboratory[13] throws a sharper focus on the educational significance of some of the psi tests in the schoolroom. In this research ESP tests carried out in the classroom, using a clairvoyance technique, showed highly significant *positive* results when pupil and teacher liked each other. But when there was a combination of dislike or disapproval on the part of both teacher and pupil, the scoring rate was as far below mean chance expectation as the positive group had scored above. Here the test revealed that psi itself was functioning under both extremes of relations, but that the psi-missing tendency was diverting it into a negative deviation when the interpersonal relations were negative. We must be cautious in interpreting these results and generalizing from them, since the experiments are still new (even though successful repetitions are already in hand as this book goes to the printer). It would, however, be entirely safe to say that, if found to have general application, these findings will have great significance for the future study of many interpersonal relationships, both in and beyond the schoolroom.

IV. Anthropology's Contact with Psi

In the analysis and evaluation of folk beliefs and practices in the comparative study of different human cultures, social anthropology has often come up against the problem of appraisal of material suggesting psi phenomena. The relationship suggested is that psi manifestations appear more prominent the less literate and scientifically sophisticated the culture. The tendency, therefore, has been to look for a predominance of psi in socially more primitive areas.

For the most part the anthropologist has been unable to evaluate the practices and beliefs that appear to involve psi functions. Consequently more or less under the restraining pressure of his own culture, he has been inclined to discount any such capacity as psi. Usually, therefore, such claims and manifestations have been attributed to credulity, illusion, and fraud.

In terms of actual work already done, only one cultural study can be mentioned here, one that was made on the Australian aborigines. The anthropologist, Elkins, of Sidney, has for many years called attention to the beliefs and practices of the aborigines as giving what appears to be, on the surface, evidence of ESP.[14] Partly under his inspiration and supervision two investigations of the aborigines have been made, one carrying over to the experimental situation the standard psi tests developed in the university laboratory for the white race[15] and the other attempting to adapt the testing techniques to the folkways of the aborigines.

As it turned out, the use of the standard techniques more or less as they are used in the university laboratory proved to be the more

LIBRARY ST. MARY'S COLLEGE

successful in getting significant results. Although the conditions were necessarily exploratory as regards full-scale precautions, significant results were obtained by Rose in ESP but not in PK tests. The tests, however, were given to aborigines who had already been to a considerable extent adjusted to the white man's culture and there was not in all cases entire purity of stock. In the second study the effort was made to adapt the standard test to aboriginal customs for the purpose of carrying the program to a more purely original cultural setting. This effort, however, remains unfinished and needs further exploration, as indeed does the whole frontier of anthropology as it touches on the presence of psi in the experience of many peoples in many lands.

In spite of a certain interest on the part of the research worker in parapsychology in the possibility that in some little known culture there will yet be found some special development of psi capacity, such a hope when critically examined could gain little encouragement from the available literature of anthropology. Even the tales of marvelous psychic mysteries in India and Tibet lose much of their impressiveness when objective accounts are obtained from different observers. It is unwise to rely wholly upon any anecdotal account, be it positive or negative, since we can well afford to be on guard against the selective bias of the mechanistic culture in which the anthropologist himself was educated.

There is also a question of what value psi test methods might have in aiding the anthropological field worker in his operations. It is important to make a better estimate than can be made by relying on the observer's mere personal impression as to whether, let us say, the witch doctor does possess the exceptional powers he claims. Many of these powers as reported would seem clearly to involve psi capacity. If the anthropologist considered it worth while most of the claims could be brought to experimental test and the question settled. Here, then, the question arises as to what kind of a test would be fair to the medicine man's claims. A bad test, of course, would be wholly misleading and would be worse than none at all. But it should be possible, with adequate knowledge both of the culture concerned and of the methods used in other areas of parapsychology research, for the anthropologist to make appropriate test adaptations to suit the field conditions of his quest.   Enough has been accomplished in the single example given by the Australian work to justify this confidence.

V. *The Biology of Psi*

The fact that psi capacity is a part of the living organism, of course, places it within the broad field of biology.   Biologists in America have not as yet given the field of parapsychology much attention, but in view of their preoccupation almost exclusively with the physical aspects of living nature this state of indifference is to be expected.   Naturally, the mechanistic philosophy which dominates reflective thought in the field makes it hard for them to look objectively at data that seem to disagree with that view as a complete theory of life.

But, as we indicated in Chapter 5, certain phenomena of animal behavior, for which no known physical explanation is forthcoming, have for centuries presented puzzling problems to biology.   Conspicuous among these and very difficult to ignore is the manner in which many species of birds in migratory flight or seasonal transition find their way over enormous distances.   Zoologists have for many years been familiar, too, with the fact that certain species are able to return successfully after being taken to points long distances from home.   Almost all types of domestic animals have in some instances been reported capable of finding their way home under a variety of circumstances that seem to leave no room for the application of any known sensory mode of guidance as a sufficient explanation.   Many exploratory experiments in animal homing, especially with mice and with certain species of birds but also to some extent with cats and dogs, have added further to the stock of information.   The results are sufficiently unexplainable by sensory perception to make the hypothesis of ESP highly relevant, for if man himself can sometimes in some way be influenced at a distance by occurrences, for example, at his home (a fire, a family illness, or other tragedy) it is reasonable to consider the possibility of the other animals likewise having some such capacity in sufficiently reliable degree to guide them in the choice of the direction they must take to find their way home.   At any rate, something does quite evidently guide them, and nothing else among experimentally established hypotheses except ESP itself seems possible to account for the majority of the occurrences.

Much attention in recent years has been given to various hypotheses put together out of complex bits of fact and theory derived from modern science to explain the navigation of homing birds. Combination theories have been devised involving the earth's magnetism, coriolis force, and the possibility that birds may have unknown but extremely sensitive sensory mechanisms capable of responding to these terrestrial influences. There are similar complex hypotheses concerning the influence of the sun, one of them involving the equivalent of an accurate chronometer in the bird. These speculatively assume that the bird makes delicate measurements of sun arc and angle and arrives at a judgment of position and direction as effectively as the trained and equipped navigator.[15a] These fantastic hypotheses, however, have lost rather than gained support from the extensive efforts to test them. Accordingly, ESP remains as the only possible hypothesis which has already had some verification. For application to these phenomena of distance orientation in animals the ESP hypothesis awaits crucial tests to decide whether it is *the* explanation instead of merely the only possible one known. (For other references to the literature see Chapter 5 or the list in the Matthews book.[15a])

The presence of psi in the few animals that have been experimentally investigated thus far gives considerable point to the ESP hypothesis in connection with the phenomena of animal behavior discussed above. As mentioned in Chapter 5, exploratory tests of ESP have been successfully carried out on one horse, two dogs, and quite a number of cats. The cat work is more recent and better controlled; in fact, it complies with the higher standards of verification, and although the results are only marginally significant, they have been confirmed to the extent of being successfully repeated by the same investigator.

The biologist, locked up as he is in his mechanistic framework of thought, is not likely to consider an ESP hypothesis for any phenomena of animal behavior on anything like equal terms with even the most fantastic sensory explanation. But this situation is obviously a temporary one in the evolution of biological thinking. There is a growing realization that this same metaphysical assumption (of physicalism) is withholding from examination the more basic factors in the organizational and directive forces in the living organism, factors in the determination of behavior, of consciousness, and of the entire personality.[16] Eventually more attention will be paid to the break-through made by parapsychology into the unexplored regions of nature to which access has been barred by the restricting dogmatism of physicalistic science. The resulting liberation might be expected to open a little further the frontier between parapsychology and biology.

Oddly enough we see today a reversal of the role of the biologist from that which he played a hundred years ago when, new facts in hand, he assailed the prevailing (though unproved) theological theory of the origin of species. Today it is the biologist who is holding out for the prevailing (but equally unproved) theory—in this case a mechanistic theory of life; while it is the parapsychologist who, new facts in hand, is presenting a challenge to a traditional assumption. Time, as the history of biology itself so well illustrates, is on the side of the facts.

VI. Physiological Explorations in Parapsychology

As a functioning part of the organism psi clearly has some kind of direct relation with the physiological system. Certainly the manifestation of psi in all the forms thus far recognized would have to involve the nervous system in particular and the organism in general to some extent. While we must leave the fundamental principles of this interaction to a much later point of research, the efforts to study the more accessible aspects of the involvement of psi in physiology may be discussed here on the basis of work already done.

Most of the psi experiments involving a physiological aspect have been exploratory efforts to influence the scoring rate by means of drugs. Both in ESP tests and in PK the effect of narcotic drugs, when used in heavy dosage, has been to interfere with positive scoring and produce "chance" results.[17,18] There has been at least one report, however, that the use of a moderate amount of alcohol (with a subject accustomed to it) had the effect of raising the scoring level.[19] The effect of a heavy dosage of the narcotic, sodium amytal, on ESP scoring was to lower a positive scoring rate to mean chance expectation. On PK tests the effect was first to increase the scoring rate and then with increased dosage to lower it. Caffein had, in general, the effect of raising the scoring level, not only in counteracting the effect of narcotic drugs (sodium amytal) but in offsetting drowsiness and fatigue. In PK tests the effect appeared as an unusual maintenance of scoring level as against a sharp decline of scoring rate in the control.[18]

Other drugs have been tried in connection with ESP tests, but thus far only with suggestive results. The effect of the stimulant drug, dexedrine, was mixed, the card test showing a decline and tests using picture targets giving improved scoring, while amytal again seemed to produce a decline.[20]

No settled conclusion has followed the exploratory inquiries on physiological states induced by drugs in connection with ESP tests, although it seems safe to accept the general impression that narcotic drugs in sufficient dosage do interfere with the subject's scoring performance in tests. Such results are, of course, to be expected in view of the known effects of these drugs upon other functions also involved in the subject's performance in the tests. There need not even be any effect of the drug upon psi capacity itself to bring about the results reported.

Only small beginnings have been made upon the important and more fundamental question of the relation of psi to the physiological functioning of the nervous system. A few beginning explorations have been made regarding the possibility of a relation between a subject's ESP scores and his electroencephalogram as recorded during the time of testing. Interesting associations have been indicated by unpublished studies that are awaiting confirmation. There is as yet, however, no evidence to suggest any basic relation, and here, as with the question of drug effects, it is necessary to remember that other functions besides psi are involved in the test and may be responsible for the effects obtained.

Other physiological measurements have been introduced to explore the range of involvement of the psi function in action. Among these introductory researches there has been an effort made to discover whether psi varies with blood pressure, with changes in skin resistance (psychogalvanic response),[19] with atmospheric pressure, and with difference in reaction time. The results have at least shown the applicability of such methods in the field of parapsychological research, but for the most part the work so far done has been highly exploratory.

Challenging problems have risen out of observations on psi effects connected with various kinds of special physiological states. The subject may have been recovering from concussion[21] or experiencing euphoria following childbirth.[22] The suggestion has been that some advantage might be found for the operation of psi under these conditions. Likewise, there have been preliminary inquiries into possible associations of psi with brain surgery (lobotomy) and the effects of shock therapy. None of the exploratory efforts have shown a significant relation.

One of the needs of the present stage, so far as the "physiology of psi" is concerned, is for more case reports from the various clinics around the world concerning the occurrence of spontaneous psi in connection with special physiological states. Cases on record regarding the psi effects surrounding death, deep anesthesia, coma, shock, and the like have already suggested there may be much to learn here about the place of psi in the organismic scheme. The study of these clues should orient the research worker on some very pertinent investigations in the future.

VII. The Psi Frontier on Medicine

No sharp distinction is drawn between the subject of discussion in this section and that of the section on psychiatry. Neither, for that matter, will there be a very clear-cut distinction between this section and that on biology. However, some research efforts remain for presentation which are essentially medical or have a distinctive bearing on medicine.

It is far too early yet to try to say how much psi is involved in the problems and practice of medicine. On the other hand, we can present a fairly good case to indicate that it has something to do with it.

Two lines of approach converge upon the general topic under discussion. One, which follows the case-study method so familiar to medicine, presents an unsolved problem or, rather, a large problem-area of concern to that field. A great wealth of medical case material from several departments of that science raises the question whether a direct subjective influence can be exerted over organic functions. Many different branches of medical inquiry have come to recognize the importance of psychological factors in the patient, factors described as anxieties, tensions, stress, spirit, or morale, or by other general terms reflecting attitudes. The success of a very exploratory psychosomatic medicine in dealing with organic disorders through the correction of attitudes has added to the empirical support for the idea that the state of mind has determinative influence over the state of the body. No advance as yet, however, has indicated how such different states can interact. In other words, it is difficult to conceive of these effects in familiar terms of causality.

Meanwhile, from the areas of unlicensed practice and unorthodox methods of healing come another collection of case reports claiming cures as a consequence of faith or other purposive attitudes of the patient.

So much for the more clinical and anecdotal approach. It serves to raise the question and it helps, sometimes at least, to point the way toward further investigation. From the other line of study bearing upon this problem of the role of psi in medicine, however, comes a more definite direction and impulse to the suggested line of thought. This approach has yielded something of an experimental answer to the question raised from the case impressions referred to; the question of whether there might be a direct action of mental upon physiological function, of conscious experience upon organic operations.

The line of thought begins with the PK researches, with the fact that under proper circumstances a person can, to a slight degree at least, influence moving physical bodies in the immediate environment. We naturally infer from these data that some sort of general function must be involved. No one would want to limit the findings to the actual dice-throwing tests on which the first work was carried out. Nature did not develop PK to throw dice, so the question is: "What else can PK do?" Knowing so little about it as we do, it is better to take very short steps in our inferences and leave until later the question we may most wish to have answered eventually—the question of the extent to which the psi function can aid the individual in his resistance to disease.

From the point of view of basic research it is better to ask if the effect demonstrated on inanimate cubes can be demonstrated similarly on living tissues.   Some exploratory researches have already been made on this next step following the establishment of PK.   We must label them all as definitely exploratory, in contrast to the researches on which the establishment of PK rests. As a rule, however, there must always be a beginning suggestion or two to stimulate scientific investigation.   In this case these hints already obtained are no less promising than any other.   We may one day come to appreciate some of the seemingly foolish little ventures that start new lines of inquiry even more highly than we will the more patently justifiable experiments that eventually verify the hypothesis.

One effort to move the PK problem into the realm of the living consisted of substituting living mobile cells for dice, the experimenter trying to influence the swimming direction of a paramecium under a low-power microscope.[23]   Another represents the effort by a worker to influence the rate of germination of spores counted under the microscope.   A third involves an attempt to influence the rate of growth of a culture of bacteria by direct mental action.   In all these explorations control tests were made for quantitative comparison, and all were reported successful. They are, we strongly emphasize, unconfirmed introductory inquiries and have only the value of inviting repetition.   But no science can afford to forget the great oaks of scientific advance begin with the tiny acorns of small unconfirmed exploratory bits like these.

Most persistently investigated in this area of research has been the claim of direct mental influence on the germination of seeds or the growth of seedlings.   The green-thumb theory, as the belief in the direct mental influence of the gardener on his plants has been called, was first brought to test by comparing an experimental section of a plot of germinating seeds with another section serving as a control.[24]   The reported success has been repeated informally and under a variety of auspices, some of them religious; but reliably controlled efforts have not as yet been conclusive.   It remains a good question whether in these tests the psychological requirements for the use of PK have been adequately met and no conclusions are in order until more thorough and exhaustive work has been conducted.

If, now, we bring together the two lines of convergent exploratory data, what do we have? There are problems in medicine that seem to call for the operation of some sort of direct action of mind on the tissues or the invading organisms. Cures are reported that might best be explained by the operation of a hypothetical psychokinetic factor. On the lines of research leading from the original PK researches, which *are* conclusive, through explorations with organic matter, where no conclusion can yet be drawn, the way has been opened for investigations that should bring out what facts there are concerning the extent of mental action along the range of the health-disease continuum. Those who face the stern realities of medical limitations in this vast area involving so large a share of the illness of mankind will appreciate the need for a forthright cautious investigation.

VIII. *Parapsychology and Religion*

The doctrines of religion are based upon what are called spiritual realities as distinguished from physical laws and operations. In terms of methods as discussed in Chapter 2 the foundations of religion rest upon personal experience or spontaneous case material. Even on the most fundamental question in all religions, that of whether there is a valid basis of spiritual reality, the case from the viewpoint of evidence rests upon individual testimony unconfirmed by experimental study.

The relation of parapsychology to religion, then, is obviously a very close one. The establishment of psi as an extraphysical capacity provides at least a limited experimental confirmation for this elemental claim of all the religions. (The relation is not altered by the fact that the need for this experimental confirmation has not been widely recognized by religious leadership; but we may recall that the introduction of experimental methods in other great practices and disciplines was similarly unsolicited.) If it is correct to define parapsychology as the science dealing with nonphysical personal agency, it is hard to see what legitimate problem or claim of religion would not, if it were brought to the point of careful investigation, belong to the domain of that science. This would make the relation of parapsychology to religion something like that of physics to engineering or biology to medicine.

This close relation may be seen to be a natural or logical one. Religious beliefs have grown up out of the experiences of the race and especially those commonly regarded as miraculous or supernatural. These more unexplainable occurrences would be expected to include a large portion of psi phenomena and the characteristics of psi would thus tend to dominate the character and coloration of religious thought. It is natural therefore that not only the divinities of the different religions but many of their principal human representatives as well (prophets, priests, and others) have been credited with extraphysical powers both to perceive beyond the sensory range and to influence the world of matter. These are, of course, the very capacities under investigation in parapsychology, these powers that have been characterized as "spiritual" in the language of religion.

In general the history of the convergence of science and religion has been one in which existing doctrines of religion have been compelled to give way to the contrary findings of science. Views of the origin of the earth and of man, conceptions of the nature of disease, and especially of mental disorder, have all been corrected by the more reliable knowledge deriving from scientific inquiry. Now, however, in its confirmation of the presence of a nonphysical or spiritual element in personality it would seem that science has for the first time made a positive contribution to the ground held by religion. In refuting the counterclaim of the mechanistic theory of man, the results even of the psi investigations already made have undermined religion's most menacing opposition.

The Hypothesis of Spirit Survival

Thus far we have been speaking of very general relations between parapsychology and religion. By taking a specific problem of religion on which actual research has been done we can more pointedly illustrate the overlap of the fields, though it should be stated in advance that the problem is not yet solved. The ques-

tion to be considered is that of whether there is a spiritual component of the individual that survives the death of the body.

By way of background it should be recalled that the belief in
some form of spirit survival is found in almost all religions. What
is more, this belief has been supported by more than the mere
authority of dogma. Religious literature and practice have generally presented the claim that the assumed discarnate agencies
can communicate with the living. While in the more organized
and intellectual religious systems communication is held to be
limited to authorized representatives of church or sect, in certain
developments of religious belief it is held that unauthorized individuals may, spontaneously or through special development,
acquire the capacity to intermediate between the discarnate world
and the living. These individuals, *mediums,* have been supposed
to be able to hear the voices of spirits and to see them when others
cannot. In a state of trance the medium has been believed by
spiritists to allow his bodily organism to be an instrument of speech
or writing through which discarnate individuals can communicate.

While at first the modern religious movement known as Spiritualism was an informal and somewhat disorganized one, its claims
of communication with the discarnate eventually attracted enough
scholarly attention to bring the problem under investigation. Interest in this problem was a large factor in the establishment of
the societies for psychical research; no existing academic or other
organization was prepared to take up the question. For the most
part the pioneer investigations made were conducted by scholars
from one or another of the established fields of study.

The question itself was simple and clear-cut: Can reliable evidence be produced that a personality can manifest itself as still
actively existing after the death of its body? The evidence that
had invited scientific attention was chiefly that given through
mediumship. It became necessary, then, to study this claim of
mediumship under conditions which would, as far as possible,
screen out alternative interpretations, such as fraud on the part of
the medium, loose interpretation on the part of the sitter (the
person visiting the medium), and the use of cues or guiding information obtainable during the sessions. Procedures were
adopted to exclude to a reasonable degree the possibility that the

medium could by normal sensory or rational methods come by the knowledge she communicated to the sitter. By locating the two in different rooms and relying upon stenographic records of the medium's utterances, the sitter could be located physically nearby and still not hear the communications intended for him. Thus the records could later be given to him along with the records of the other sittings without his knowing which had been meant for him. In this way any individual tendency toward a biased interpretation could be neutralized by the method of analysis. Also, the question of chance coincidence could be dealt with by this procedure by evaluating a sitter's responses to his own record (by means of those he made on others) and applying a statistical method to the scores obtained.[25,26]

The countertheory that could not be ruled out, however, was that of the medium's own psi capacity to acquire information either telepathically from the sitter or from other sources by means of clairvoyance. As a matter of fact, the amount of information conveyed in ESP card tests by the more outstanding subjects would exceed the knowledge contributed in well-controlled sessions with the medium in trance.

Thus far the investigation of mediumship by scientific method has not got beyond this difficulty of interpretation. There is reasonably good indication that knowledge has been obtained through mediumistic utterances that would have to be considered parapsychical in its origin. There is no way known as yet to test the hypothesis that the source of the knowledge shown is discarnate.

The establishment of psi itself has naturally somewhat improved the status of the hypothesis of spirit survival. The possibility of the survival of a spiritual factor in man seems the more reasonable since the establishment of such a property in the living. At the same time, the psi investigations have to such a degree extended the possibilities of what the medium could do through her own powers that it is now not easy to see how anything which could be communicated through the medium could be proved to have been beyond her own capacities. In view of the fact that the whole conception of discarnate existence, agency, and communication, is in itself based on the assumption of parapsychical powers, we have to suppose that much the same kind and degree of such capacities would be needed for spirit communication as would be required by the medium to get the information or produce the observed effects by means of her own powers. It is in this state of ambiguity that the question of spirit survival has to be left for the present.

The researches in parapsychology have, on the whole, opened a new approach to the problems of religion, problems which are of surpassing importance to mankind. Whether the impulse comes primarily from religionists or scientists will not matter if the pursuit of careful inquiry to these great issues is pressed with the vigor and forthrightness they deserve. The issues are too great to be left only for the preliminary methods of inquiry which they have had in the past. Nothing but the most definitive procedures and standards of research should be taken as adequate for conclusion where questions of human destiny are at stake.

IX. *The Philosophy of Psi*

Philosophy should probably be considered as bordering on all branches of the domain of science. Its relation to a new science, however, is likely to be especially close and involved. Fortunately for parapsychology, some of the leading philosophers of the western world have taken an active interest in its problems from the very beginning of psi investigations in the days of Henry Sidgwick and William James.

Where the actual investigations of parapsychology have most definitely crossed the borders of academic philosophy is in the investigation of the psychophysical problem. This is an issue of long standing in the field of philosophy, variously characterized as the mind-body problem or the question of the place of man in nature. As we have indicated, the focus of parapsychology, too, is on this question although it is not usually stated in that way. In the investigation of phenomena of human personality that challenge physical explanation the inquiry is naturally at the outset one of whether any sort of nonphysical operations may be actually and adequately demonstrated. If so, a *scientific* solution can be found to the mind-body problem of philosophy.

If, then, in further parapsychological investigations the experi-

mental studies bring out clearly the active *inter*-relationships between the nonphysical function of psi and the physical environment with which its demonstration is concerned, a second advance
into the mind-body relation will have been made; that is to say
that not only have both physical and nonphysical operations been
shown to occur in the human individual, but they will also have
been demonstrated to be *inter*active.   As it is, the manifestation
of psi through physical effects and records makes it necessary to
assume interaction of psi and physical processes.

In a word, science is closing in on a question on which much of
the philosophic thought of the western world in recent centuries
has been expended.   Thus far the results of the psi researches in
establishing a nonphysical interaction between subject and object
do not confirm any one of the specific philosophical solutions
(dualisms and monisms) that have been speculatively proposed.
The results indicate, as scientific conclusions do in such cases, a
comparative and complementary rather than an absolute distinction between the areas concerned (mind and matter).   The contrast between the physical and nonphysical, while very important
and full of meaning for psychology and related fields, cannot be
regarded as more than a relative one.   Some degree of psychophysical unity may at the same time be inferred in view of the
evidence of interaction.

But if parapsychology as a science has removed one of the problems of philosophy, it has produced some new ones too.   It seems
reasonable to say that the philosophical challenge of the evidence
for precognition offers as baffling a question as any yet encountered
in human thought.   It is true many of the questions raised by
precognition (e.g., its clash with causality and with volitional
freedom) will have to be answered by the expansion of knowledge
gained through experimentation.   However, in the search for such
knowledge a great deal will depend upon the rational analysis of
the problems raised and the intellectual adjustments that will have
to follow the acceptance of this newly discovered property of the
human mind.

It seems safe to say that many formulations of philosophical
theory based upon past conceptions of human nature will have
to be recast in the light of the new facts on the presence of a non-

physical element in the human makeup. There may be many consequences to the ethical, political, and religious thinking of men to follow from the altered picture of the nature of man which the new facts provide. The border, then, between parapsychology and philosophy will probably be one involved in active exchange and mutual stimulation for a long and indefinite future.

References

1. LINTOTT, G. A. M.: Some observations on so-called water divining. *Guy's Hosp. Gaz.*, June 24, 1933.
2. MCMAHAN, E. A.: A review of the evidence for dowsing. *J. Parapsychol.*, *11*:175–190, 1947.
3. RHINE, J. B.: Some exploratory tests in dowsing. *J. Parapsychol.*, *14*:278–286, 1950.
4. CADORET, R. J.: The reliable application of ESP. *J. Parapsychol.*, *19*:203–227, 1955.
5. SHULMAN, R.: A study of card-guessing in psychotic subjects. *J. Parapsychol.*, *2*:95–106, 1938.
6. BATES, K. E., and NEWTON, M.: An experimental study of ESP capacity in mental patients. *J. Parapsychol.*, *15*:271–277, 1951.
7. WEST, D. J.: ESP tests with psychotics. *J. Soc. Psychical Res.*, *36*: 619–623, 1952.
8. HUMPHREY, B. M.: ESP tests with mental patients before and after electroshock treatment. *J. Soc. Psychical Res.*, *37*:259–265, 1954.
9. EISENBUD, J.: Psychiatric contributions to parapsychology: A review. *J. Parapsychol.*, *13*:247–262, 1949.
10. VAN BUSSCHBACH, J. G.: An investigation of extrasensory perception in school children. *J. Parapsychol.*, *17*:210–214, 1953.
11. VAN BUSSCHBACH, J. G.: A further report on an investigation of ESP in school children. *J. Parapsychol.*, *19*:73–81, 1955.
12. VAN BUSSCHBACH, J. G.: An investigation of ESP between teacher and pupils in American schools. *J. Parapsychol.*, *20*:71–80, 1956.
13. ANDERSON, M., and WHITE, R.: Teacher-pupil attitudes and clairvoyance test results. *J. Parapsychol.*, *20*:141–157, 1956.
14. ELKINS, A. P.: *Aboriginal Men of High Degree.* Sidney, Australasian, 1944.
15. ROSE, R.: A second report on psi experiments with Australian aborigines. *J. Parapsychol.*, *19*:92–98, 1955.

15a. MATTHEWS, G. V. T.: *Bird Navigation.* London, Cambridge Univ. Press, 1955.
16. SINNOTT, E. W.: *Cell and Psyche.* Chapel Hill, Univ. North Carolina Press, 1950.
17. RHINE, J. B.: *Extrasensory Perception.* Boston, Bruce Humphries, 1934.
18. AVERILL, R. L., and RHINE, J. B.: Effect of alcohol upon performance in PK tests. *J. Parapsychol.,* 9:32–41, 1945.
19. BRUGMANS, H. J. F. W.: Some experiments in telepathy performed in the Psychological Institute of the University of Gröningen. *Compte-Rendu du Premier Congrès International des Recherches Psychiques,* 1921.
20. CADORET, R. J.: The effect of amytal and dexedrine on ESP performance. *J. Parapsychol.,* 17:259–274, 1953.
21. SCHMEIDLER, G. R.: Rorschach and ESP scores of patients suffering from cerebral concussions. *J. Parapsychol.,* 16:80–89, 1952.
22. GERBER, R., and SCHMEIDLER, G. R.: An investigation of relaxation and of acceptance of the experimental situation as related to ESP scores in maternity patients. *J. Parapsychol.,* 21:47–57, 1957.
23. RICHMOND, N.: Two series of PK tests on paramecia. *J. Soc. Psychical Res.,* 37:577–587, 1952.
24. VASSE, P.: Experiences de germination de plantes. *Rev. Métapsychique,* New Series No. 12, 223–225, 1950.
25. PRATT, J. G.: *Towards a Method of Evaluating Mediumistic Material.* Boston, Boston Soc. Psychical Res., Bull. 23, 1936.
26. PRATT, J. G., and BIRGE, W. R.: Appraising verbal test material in parapsychology. *J. Parapsychol.,* 12:236–256, 1948.

Additional Reading

BARRETT, W. F., and BESTERMAN, T.: *The Divining Rod,* London, Methuen, 1926.
BROAD, C. D.: Philosophical implications of foreknowledge. *Proc. Aristotelian Soc.,* 16:177–209, 1937.
CARINGTON, W.: The quantitative study of trance personalities: New series, I. *Proc. Soc. Psychical Res.,* 45:223–251, 1939.
DEVEREUX, G. (ed.): Psychoanalysis and the Occult. New York, Internat. Univ. Press, 1953.
DUCASSE, C. J.: The philosophical importance of "psychic phenomena." *J. Philosophy,* 51:810–823, 1954.

EDITORIAL: ESP, PK and the survival hypothesis. *J. Parapsychol.*, 7:223–227, 1943.

EDITORIAL: Hypnosis and ESP. *Parapsychol. Bull.*, No. 24, 1951.

EDITORIAL: Hypnotism, "graduate" of parapsychology. *J. Parapsychol.*, 6:159–163, 1942.

EDITORIAL: Parapsychology and psychiatry. *J. Parapsychol.*, 13:143–150, 1949.

EDITORIAL: The question of practical application of parapsychical abilities. *J. Parapsychol.*, 9:77–79, 1945.

EVANS, C. C., and OSBORN, E.: An experiment in the electro-encephalography of mediumistic trance. *J. Soc. Psychical Res.*, 36:588–596, 1952.

FREUD, S.: Dreams and the occult, in *New Introductory Lectures on Psycho-analysis*. New York, Norton, 1933.

GRELA, J. J.: Effect on ESP scoring of hypnotically induced attitudes. *J. Parapsychol.*, 9:194–202, 1945.

KATY, E., and PAULSON, P.: A brief history of the divining rod in the United States, I. *J. Am. Soc. Psychical Res.*, 42:119–131, 1948; II. *J. Amer. Soc. Psychical Res.*, 43:3–18, 1949.

KNOWLES, F. W.: Some investigations into psychic healing. *J. Am. Soc. Psychical Res.*, 48:21–26, 1954.

MUNDLE, C. W. K.: Some philosophical perspectives for parapsychology. *J. Parapsychol.*, 16:257–272, 1952.

MURPHY, G.: An outline of survival evidence. *J. Am. Soc. Psychical Res.*, 39:2–34, 1945.

MURPHY, G.: Difficulties confronting the survival hypothesis. *J. Am. Soc. Psychical Res.*, 39:67–94, 1945.

MURPHY, G.: Field theory and survival. *J. Am. Soc. Psychical Res.*, 39:181–209, 1945.

MURPHY, G.: Spontaneous telepathy and the problem of survival. *J. Parapsychol.*, 7:50–60, 1943.

OTANI, S.: Relations of mental set and change of skin resistance to ESP. *J. Parapsychol.*, 19:164–170, 1955.

PRICE, H. H.: Survival and the idea of "another world." *Proc. Soc. Psychical Res.*, 50:1–25, 1953.

RHINE, J. B.: Hypnotic suggestion in PK tests. *J. Parapsychol.*, 10:126–140, 1946.

RHINE, J. B.: *Telepathy and Human Personality* (The Tenth F. W. H. Myers Memorial Lecture). London, Society for Psychical Research, 1950.

RHINE, J. B.:   The question of spirit survival.   *J. Am. Soc. Psychical Res.*, *43*:43–58, 1949.

RICHMOND, K.:   Experiments on the relief of pain.   *J. Soc. Psychical Res.*, *33*:194–207, 1946.

SALTMARSH, H. F.:   *Evidence of Personal Survival from Cross Correspondences.*   London, Bell, 1938.

WALLWORK, S. C.:   ESP experiments with simultaneous electro-encephalographic recordings.   *J. Soc. Psychical Res.*, *36*:697–701, 1952.

WEST, D. J.   *Psychical Research Today.*   London, Duckworth, 1954.

WOODRUFF, J. L., and DALE, L. A.:   ESP function and the psychogalvanic response.   *J. Am. Soc. Psychical Res.*, *46*:62–65, 1952.

PART II

Testing Techniques

Chapter 7

Psychological Recommendations for Psi Testing

I. Right Psychological Conditions Essential

Iт is wise in looking at the problem of conducting a psi test properly to keep in mind that it is a purely psychological function that is being tested and to allow it every possible psychological consideration.

We may, in fact, define a proper psi test as one in which the essential objective conditions are adequately provided and thereafter taken for granted, allowing first emphasis to be placed on the effectiveness of the test in demonstrating psi. In short, it would not be a psi test if it were not to go beyond the mere precautionary requirements. Rather, it must first of all meet the psychological conditions under which psi can operate. While the establishment of the occurrence of psi was at issue it was difficult to press the point of these intangible requirements. But now that that has been accomplished, it would be unreasonable to consider as an adequate test of psi anything less than one properly calculated to evoke the ability to be tested as well as to measure it safely when evoked.

II. Influence of the Experimenter

When we begin to think of psi testing in these more psychological terms we appreciate the failures and difficulties all the more because we better understand them. Most conspicuous, perhaps, among failures is the fact that some experimenters have found themselves unable to conduct successful psi experiments; that is, when they have gone through the standard testing routines with their subjects they obtained only chance results. In most such cases no thoroughgoing effort was made to test a wide range of subjects, a variety of test conditions, and other possibilities that might have led to fruitful results. But in a few instances efforts have been made that were fairly extensive in amount of time and energy expended, and still comparatively little beyond chance data was obtained. The occurrence of such failures is one serious fact to be considered in looking for the psychological requirements of a psi test.

Another major difficulty can be seen in the fact that some experimenters after a period of earlier success in obtaining extrachance results in psi experiments have proved less effective in their later efforts. In such instances something apparently has been lost that was once a potent factor. The element most likely to change under prolonged testing would seem to be the quality of infectious enthusiasm that accompanies the initial discoveries of the research worker. Those who never succeed at all may, of course, be suspected of not ever having felt such contagious or communicable interest as would help to create a favorable test environment for their subjects.

Whatever the explanation—and there is no need to wait for the establishment of a theory of it—it is simply common sense for the experimenter to find out whether he is qualified before he goes far in trying to commit himself to what is necessarily an untried and uncertain professional task. In a more pioneering and amateurish stage of parapsychology, in ignorance of what the limiting factors might be, it was pardonable to explore longer and more patiently to see whether initial difficulties might be overcome. Today, however, the stage has been reached at which it can be said definitely that the experimenter himself can be a limiting factor in the test situation and, if he be, he had better find out by preliminary tests of himself *as experimenter*. The only rule to follow is that of the old motto: "Pretty is as pretty does." A psi experimenter is one who, under conditions that insure he is not fooling himself, can get results. All others should do something they *can* do well. For the truly resolute research worker this may still be in parapsychology, if he is willing and able to find the right coworkers or to turn to one of the many nontesting areas in which he can work effectively.

III. *The Psychological Needs of the Subject in Psi Tests*

But, as the facts all too plainly show, the difficulties are by no means limited to the experimenter himself. The subject, too, is an uncertain quantity. It is theoretically possible, at least, that a given subject or a given group of subjects may have no ESP ability at all. There is no way at present of absolutely knowing this, and it is better at this stage to take the much more reasonable assumption that everyone has potential ESP capacity and that there are many circumstances that affect and may inhibit the exercise of it. A great deal of evidence favors this working hypothesis of ESP as a species characteristic even though actual proof may still be lacking. This working assumption allows for and even favors the more realistic and useful view that subjects are made, not born, and that something, indeed much, may be done, especially by the experimenter himself, to develop or at least help to prepare the subject for the investigation to be made with him.

The uncertain performance of subjects in psi tests is still the major difficulty in parapsychology. Some subjects who come to the test situation and at first show no evidence of psi capacity under the conditions of the test may later prove successful under other conditions. Others may begin at a high level of scoring and as the testing continues under the same external conditions may lose their ability to give extrachance results. Such an outcome has almost always occurred when a given subject has been investigated long and continuously. High scoring subjects have always lost their ability to score above chance. This is in reality a variation of the formula that good subjects are not born but made, for it shows that good subjects can be *un*made too. Unfortunately, the kind of testing that has characterized nearly all the outstanding subjects in the history of parapsychology has resulted in the undoing of the successful performer. It seems now that the testing itself as at present conducted is lethal to the psi function, or perhaps we had better say to the capacity to demonstrate it.

It would be folly, then, to ignore the very fluid or flexible character of the function being tested in these various operations. We are not dealing with a firmly-fixed capacity that is present in some individuals and not in others; rather, we are dealing with something that exists in the individual as a delicate potential. In some persons it has been, at the time the experimenter encountered them, much further developed and more accessible to test demonstration than in others. These would be the more promising subjects. We know now, however, that the experimenter should think how he will sustain the subject's interest over the period during which he hopes to conduct his tests, how he will counteract the inhibiting influence of the test experience itself. He knows first that in monotonous test routines interest tends to wane quickly, with some individuals more quickly than with others. His skill in keeping his subjects freshly motivated will be very important. He will be very fortunate if he finds in the subject an easily sustained, long-standing interest and the qualities of personality (patience, optimism, a capacity for devotion, etc.) that will help him to keep up the flame of his own zeal to achieve a high record in the experiment. Fortunately, there have been a few such subjects, and doubtless many more can be found.

Subjects should be, of course, as far as possible selected first for their maximum interest, availability, and adaptability to the circumstances of the test, but then the experimenter's task has only fairly begun. The fine art of interpersonal relations has probably never been better put to test than it has been in the development of a finely poised sense of the challenge of a psi experiment. Here the subject is stimulated to bring out in measurable degree the manifestation of an influence he cannot consciously command, cannot even realistically feel is operating, and yet must by an act of venturesome faith believe might *possibly* exercise itself in the task to which he is committing himself. All this he must do without feeling silly or futile! In all the various subtle experiences of the human mind there are probably none more calculated to put the individual on his mettle, to exercise a supremely delicate discrimination, to sustain the most finely balanced judgment, and to maintain throughout a restrained control of the numerous sensory, mnemonic, and rational influences that tend to crowd the focus of attention. This is the stage over which the experimenter must maintain a directive influence in helping the subject to achieve his best, not just once, but over a long series of trials, through many runs, and if possible many sessions.

What wonder if it eventually fails? It should not be surprising that both subject and experimenter eventually wear out the necessary freshness of interest in the test which the demonstration of psi requires.

IV. *The Experimenter-Subject Relation in Psi Tests*

Not only must the experimenter and the subject both be prepared for the psi test, but the test and the experimental design it represents should be planned with careful understanding.   Generally speaking the shorter an experimental series can be made and still meet its requirements, the better for both experimenter and subject.   The shorter a given contribution by a given subject can be made, the better, for in long-drawn-out sessions and experimental series some important element is used up or lost.   The spontaneous interest with which the subject approaches the test may decline considerably in the course of a single run.   Although something of its freshness may be recaptured in the beginning of the succeeding run, still it is not likely ever to be quite as good as at the start.   Perhaps in time a new discovery will be made showing how to reinspire the subject for later performances and even bring about progressive improvement as the experiment continues, instead of the decline that now characterizes most experiments.   But for the present it is better to be prepared for a potential decline and prepared at the same time to see how much of the original spontaneity can be preserved—and for how long a time.   One way to help this is to make the procedure as brief, varied, and novel as the design of the experiment will allow.   The period between runs is especially important.   During this time the aim should be to recapture and restore the original zest for the experiment and thus counteract the effect of the monotony on the subjects.   The checking of the score sheets with the subject participating can be made a diverting procedure, especially by pointing out interesting effects and making optimistic interpretations.   But any diversionary hunting for added value in the data should be limited or it may tend to disperse the subject's main interest in high scoring on the target.

Perhaps the most important requirement of the experimenter is to be able to preserve and frequently renew the original lively

LIBRARY ST. MARY'S COLLEGE

impulse that brought the subject into the ESP experiment. Ideally, as already indicated, interest will grow with the good results of the earlier tests, but such interest must never be taken for granted. With this in mind plans directed at some terminal point, some over-all outcome of the experiment as a whole, can be helpful in sustaining the requisite initiative. Whenever the research calls for the maintenance of high scoring over a prolonged series, some far-viewed objective is essential to avert the normal decline effect.

No matter what the individual qualities of the experimeter and the subject may be, there is always a mutual effect of the one upon the other. It is now known that the sign of the deviation may be affected by this interpersonal relation. The subject may be highly motivated in the test even if he does not like the experimenter, but the chances are good that dislike will produce a drop in his scoring not merely to a chance average but even to a negative deviation (from the chance mean). But unless the experiment is one in which a negative deviation is anticipated and prepared for, such combinations are, of course, to be avoided.

It is fairly obvious, then, that the development of a professional job in the investigation of psi calls for the development of a profession of psi investigation. In addition to the fundamental scientific requirements, there are certain arts and skills which cannot be contributed entirely on a basis of knowledge. Experience and personal techniques will have to be developed. Presumably they can be developed in this area of relations as well as in any other in which people try to influence others. It is a point of view that must be stressed if psi is going to continue to be successfully demonstrated.

It is also necessary to search for what might be called veins of ready-made psi relations, to look for those existing social institutions in which it may be more natural than elsewhere for psi to function without need of the buildup of special subject-experimenter relations. Recent work in the public schools has brought such uniform success in tests in which the teacher serves as agent with pupils as percipients that it appears that such a vein has been found in this social stratum of the teacher-pupil relation. It appears that in this relation a rapport that facilitates the operation of ESP may already be established.   As stated, the outstanding work of this nature is that of van Busschbach of Amsterdam. The success achieved in this area encourages the hope that other such strata may be found in which the area of possibilities of ready-made psi relations can be extended.

But still another similar need is evident today, that of the development of an applied science of parapsychology.   Toward this end it is important to turn to account all that has been learned from the research of the past in the effort to increase the reliability of psi under test conditions.   It is time to concentrate attention on the problem of extending the subject's (as well as the experimenter's) control over the psi function.   This should be sought first in the discovery of more about the psychological conditions affecting psi.   It would greatly help, too, if better investigational devices could be acquired that would make the psi test more informative as it proceeds and permit the experimenter to be guided by a currently registered analysis of the subject's type of performance.   This would require elaborate but not necessarily new equipment.   It would seem possible that a degree of control might be exerted over the psi function that would make its application a fully practical possibility.

Perhaps the slowly growing awareness of the tremendous practical applications that are in store for psi may bring fresh interest to this old problem of the practical utilization of the function. With the stage of psychological understanding already reached concerning some of the major difficulties, and with the discovery of such naturally favored psi relations as the schoolroom, for example, can provide, it may remain now only for a sufficiently aroused interest to justify a full program of testing aimed at a practical utilization of psi.   Perhaps the step most needed is the development of a course for the training of professional psi investigators for a larger scale of research operations.

Additional Reading

CADORET, R. J.:   Effect of novelty in test conditions on ESP performance.   *J. Parapsychol.*, *16*:192–203, 1952.

EDITORIAL: Conditions affecting ESP.   *J. Parapsychol.*, *2*:155–159, 1938.

HUMPHREY, B. M.: *Handbook of Tests in Parapsychology.* Durham, N. C., Parapsychology Laboratory, 1948, pp. 111–116.

PRATT, J. G., and PRICE, M.: The experimenter-subject relationship in tests for ESP. *J. Parapsychol.,* 2:84–94, 1938.

PRICE, M., and RHINE, J. B.: The subject-experimenter relation in the PK test. *J. Parapsychol.,* 8:177–186, 1944.

RHINE, J. B.: Conditions favoring success in psi tests. *J. Parapsychol.,* 12:58–75, 1948.

RHINE, J. B.: *Extrasensory Perception.* Boston, Bruce Humphries, 1934, pp. 166–168.

SCHERER, W. B.: Spontaneity as a factor in ESP. *J. Parapsychol.,* 12: 126–147, 1948.

SMITH, B. M., and GIBSON, E. P.: Conditions affecting ESP performance. *J. Parapsychol.,* 5:58–86, 1941.

THOULESS, R. H.: A report on an experiment in psychokinesis with dice, and a discussion on psychological factors favoring success. *Proc. Soc. Psychical Res.,* 49:107–130, 1951.

Chapter 8

Some Basic Psi Test Procedures

I. Introduction

T HESE instructions follow the distinction between exploratory and conclusive methods made in Chapter 2. Each of these two broad stages of research naturally requires experimental procedures appropriate to it. This presentation of techniques takes for granted a general acquaintance with Part I of the book. Chapter 7 dealing with psychological conditions affecting psi is of special importance. A glossary of terms is given on pages 207–210.

Four basic test procedures are described. They are the most widely used and will cover most of the needs the readers of this volume will likely have. These procedures are themselves comparatively easily adapted to a wider range of special situations. The procedures given are for tests of clairvoyance, of general extrasensory perception, of precognition, and of psychokinesis. They are described first in the form appropriate for exploratory experiments. Later, in a separate section, precautions required for conclusive experimentation are added for all four types of tests.

The aim is to present test instructions that will enable the student or professional worker to start his own experimenting in whatever general area of parapsychology or its application he may choose. As the experimenter continues to the point at which he may wish to know about other methods, he will already have become acquainted with research literature in which they are to be found.* He will have made the acquaintance of the Hum-

---

* E.g., *The Journal of Parapsychology*, published by the Duke University Press, Durham, N. C.

phrey *Handbook of Tests in Parapsychology*.[†] In matters of method and research design, we shall be glad to consult with readers who desire assistance.

II. Exploratory Psi Tests

A. General Instructions

Much can be said here that applies in a general way to all the test procedures and that would otherwise have to be repeated over and over in the specific procedures to follow. For example, the level of precaution assumed for exploratory tests is one in which it is taken for granted that the experimenter merely wants to be reasonably sure that in the tests the subject has done what he was supposed to do. Precautions are taken against the more likely errors or counterhypotheses, assuming normally careful observation and reporting. It is all done on the assumption that final conclusions will require a more cautious type of experiment. The methods given here will serve the inquirer well enough to justify his going on to the next, more safeguarded stage. Some at the start will not want to take as much trouble as these procedures require. Others may want to begin (though they are advised not to) further up the scale of precaution. In the various clinical, educational, practical, and recreational applications of psi tests the present level of controls will be generally adequate.

Test Cards. It will save trouble to begin with the standard pack of ESP test cards (or a near-equivalent) which has long been in use. ESP cards have been kept commercially available for the convenience of workers in the field.[*] The pack consists of twenty-five cards, normally with five of each of five geometric designs: star, circle, square, cross, waves. It is referred to as a *closed* pack when it has this even distribution of symbols or an *open* pack if the cards have been arranged in random order regardless of whether the numbers of symbols are equal.

No matter how well printed test cards of any kind may be, they

---

[†] Published at Durham, N. C., by the Parapsychology Laboratory of Duke University, 1948.

[*] The authorized distributors for the ESP test cards in this country are The Haines House of Cards, Norwalk, Ohio, and their agents.

should not be considered free from identifying marks, even when new. Even in exploratory tests of ESP the cards can just as well be kept out of sight of the person being tested, unless the test provides other safeguards against sensory cues (as some do). It is easy to set up some kind of opaque screen to conceal the cards in even the most informal test.

Shuffling. Ordinary shuffling methods will do sufficiently well for introductory experiments, but it is best to develop a simple ritual of shuffling that insures that this part of the procedure is not overlooked. We suggest that a minimum of four dovetail shuffles be given the pack followed by a cut made with a knife or thumbnail. This shuffling should be done just before the test is to begin (except, of course, in a precognition experiment) and should be done behind whatever screen is set up to render the pack invisible to the subject. The cards are kept by the experimenter (behind the screen) until the run through the pack is finished.

Recording. The use of a prepared record sheet is very advantageous. A standard form of ESP record sheet is shown on p. 142. Some will wish to obtain already prepared forms,* while others will be able to mimeograph their own supply.

The subject himself can usually make the record of his calls or "guesses." If any change has to be made it is better not to erase the error but to draw a line through it and add the correction. When the call record for a run is completed, if the cards have not already been recorded it will reduce the likelihood of error to cover up the subject's call record while the card order is being put down by the experimenter. Better still, the two records can be made on different sheets; if not, the record sheet may be folded and the call record turned down during the card recording. For very preliminary testing this precaution is not to be taken seriously. At a more careful stage, however, it will assure the experimenter that he is not allowing his attention to be distracted by the symbol recorded in the adjoining column as he watches to see whether a hit or a miss was made. When the recording is completed immediate checking for hits is desirable in general, and

---

* The Parapsychology Laboratory of Duke University will supply ESP record sheets in pads of 50 sheets.

ESP RECORD SHEET

No._____

Subject _H. Pearce_   Experiment _Subseries D (copy)_

Observer _J.G.P. & J.B.R._   Date _Mar. 12-13, '34_

Type of Test _Clairvoyance BT_   Time _____

General conditions _Distance test — 100 yards_

Use other side for remarks.   Total score_____   Avge. score_____

With ESP cards use ∧ for star, o for circle, L for square, + for cross, = for waves.

1		2		3		4		5		6		7		8		9		10	
Call	Card	Call	Card	Call	Card	Call	Card	Call	Card	Call	Card	Call	Card	Call	Card	Call	Card	Call	Card
∧	∧	o	L	o	=	+	+	o	=	L	L								
o	L	L	∧	=	o	∧	L	∧	∧	∧	+								
o	L	∧	L	∧	∧	o	o	L	=	L	o								
=	=	L	o	+	o	L	o	∧	∧	∧	∧								
+	∧	+	∧	=	+	+	+	+	=	+	L								
=	L	∧	=	o	=	L	+	=	∧	o	o								
L	L	=	=	L	L	o	o	+	+	+	L								
L	o	=	+	∧	o	+	∧	+	+	∧	=								
∧	o	o	=	L	L	o	=	o	o	+	+								
o	o	∧	+	L	∧	∧	L	+	L	+	o								
+	+	L	+	o	o	=	∧	o	=	=	∧								
+	=	o	+	+	+	+	+	+	+	o	o								
L	L	+	=	L	L	o	L	L	+	=	=								
o	∧	L	o	+	=	=	=	o	o	o	+								
∧	∧	=	L	=	+	o	∧	∧	o	∧	∧								
L	o	o	∧	L	=	∧	o	o	o	L	+								
o	=	=	o	∧	L	∧	∧	∧	=	o	L								
=	=	∧	o	+	=	=	=	=	L	+	∧								
o	+	∧	∧	L	o	o	L	=	+	=	∧								
+	+	+	o	∧	∧	+	+	L	L	o	o								
∧	∧	L	=	=	∧	o	L	=	∧	∧	=								
+	+	+	+	L	L	+	o	∧	L	+	L								
=	=	=	∧	∧	+	∧	∧	L	L	=	=								
L	o	+	L	∧	∧	=	=	+	o	+	+								
=	+	o	L	+	+	+	=	+	∧	o	=								
12	**3**		**10**		**11**		**10**		**10**										

ESP record sheet for tests with writing or calling techniques.

In recording, use ∧ for star, o for circle, L for square, + for cross, — for waves

ESP record sheet for matching techniques.

the subject may serve as an observer—though only in that role. The recording of all scores immediately in a notebook will insure completeness in evaluating results.

Planning. If the experiment, no matter how exploratory, is given a definite (and preferably recorded) *plan,* there are certain advantages in the interpretation of results; for example, it is extremely important in making any sort of interpretation to know that all of the data are taken into account. This involves preparing in advance a paragraph of description of what is to be undertaken, how many runs are considered a suitable length for the experiment, and roughly what the objective and the experimental conditions are. If any special type of statistical evaluation is to be used on the results it should be included in the plan. The explorer, of course, need not bind himself to these precautions; in fact, he will need to decide at what stage of his procedural advance they are worth the trouble. But if he has them in mind they will likely come into use earlier.

Evaluating Results. Tables have been provided at the back of the book for the evaluation of most of the types of test results likely to be obtained from the procedures described. With each table instructions for its use are given. Some of the tables are intended to meet the beginning needs of inexperienced workers, and their use will not require any special training in statistical method. These particular tables will, of course, not be perfectly adapted to all the needs of the exploratory research worker, but as he gains experience and interest in the use of the methods, he will want to take advantage of Chapter 9 on statistical methods and thereby acquire the knowledge necessary to evaluate his own results independently with the aid of the other tables presented.

The use of the evaluation tables makes certain assumptions that are general: First, that all of the test data of a project are included. If only a certain group of runs or a selected section of the whole experiment were to be considered by itself, the value given in a table would be misleading. It is assumed, too, that the subject had only one call (or in PK one throw) per trial and that, if the subject was told of his success or failure before the end of the run, the cards were reshuffled before the next trial. The tables, likewise, are based on the assumption that it was decided in advance of how many runs the experiment would consist. If this was not done, a favorable stopping place might be chosen and a statistical correction would be needed for the value given in the tables. The tables also assume that the type of statistical analysis was planned in advance of the experiment, or at least before the data were examined in a manner that might conceivably have indicated the effect to be evaluated. Whenever the plan of the experiment leaves any leeway in the manner of analyzing the results, it is always necessary to choose the more conservative evaluation or to make an appropriate correction in the probability value.

Many explorers will want to know what the shortest satisfactory test series might be that would still allow a safe use of the tables. For very preliminary purposes a four-run test totaling 100 trials will be safe enough. For the testing of an individual's psi capacity or the exploring of a new claim or hypothesis a 20-run or 500-trial minimum would be a reasonable line to draw. It is better not to plan longer experimental series, since interest tends to wane with monotonous repetition. Short series with many innovations, even minor ones, are better and are statistically acceptable.

Preparation of Subject. In any psi test it is important that the subject not only understand what the test is for and what his part in it is to be, but he needs to be familiarized with the procedure in order that its novelty will not distract him. If cards are to be used, he should be allowed to see them before he begins and even make a few informal, off-the-record trials in order that the various symbols will come easily to mind. The names of the symbols should be used often enough for him to be able to recall them without effort. If the subject is to record his own calls, he should have the simplified way of recording made known to him, so that the recording will proceed smoothly.

Unless the subject has already developed an idea of the way he should proceed, what mental device he should try to use in the test, it is best to talk with him briefly and informally about the matter to insure that he has no confusion over what he should do. It should be explained to him, if necessary, that it would not be of any use to try to keep track of the symbols already called or to use any kind of logical system. The suggestion might be made, if it seems necessary, that the subject simply try to allow all the symbols equal access to the center of attention and in each trial he should call the symbol that seems to stand out most vividly, using his visual imagery to recall them, or, if he prefers, looking at a set of the five symbols or a picture of them as he proceeds. If any such suggestions are offered, care must be taken not to make the subject self-conscious about the test.

Above all, the subject should be encouraged to work out his own way of making his calls and a choice of test procedures may profitably be offered him as well. Minor variations allowable within the scope of the procedure introduced should be made to help to "fit the subject to the test." Making clear the elements of the procedure will bring out also whether the subject is mentally prepared for the test, whether he has proper interest, good motivation, and freedom from the many possible inhibiting conditions that may be associated with the first adjustment to a new situation. The whole concept of the psi test takes for granted that the essential psychological conditions are adequately provided.

B. ESP Tests: 1. Clairvoyance

*The BT Test.** In this test the subject tries to identify the cards as, one by one, the experimenter takes the top card from the inverted pack and holds it in a designated position. The experimenter does not look at the symbol and after the subject makes his choice the card is put face down in another position. If, as should always be done, some kind of opaque screen is used, the experimenter may hold the card against the screen until the subject makes his response. The subject may either make his calls orally or if a low screen is used he may point to one of the five symbols (e.g., as printed on the back of the box); or, again, he may keep his own written record.

Usually the test proceeds through the twenty-five cards without any attempt to check on the success of the subject, but in more introductory tests it may be desirable to stop after every five trials

---

* BT is now a widely known term for this technique. It originally meant "broken technique" as compared to DT or "down through" the *unbroken* pack. "Basic technique" would be a better designation today for it is an elementary type of procedure.

(or any other part of the total run). If anything less than the full run is made the stopping point, the whole pack should be reshuffled before the test is resumed. If a subject appears to be working hard on each trial, it is wise to break up the run into sections. At the completion of the run (or other stopping place) the experimenter should turn the pack over and record the card order, taking whatever precautions the stage of his inquiry requires. Then follows the checking for hits, at which point it is a good plan to invite the subject to watch to insure accuracy. By placing the two columns of the records side by side (the call column and the card column) the number of hits can easily be scored and should be marked on the record sheet with the total score at the bottom.

The test is essentially the same whether the standard ESP test symbols are used or whether five colors, five numbers, or some other kind of targets should be used. The test may also be done with a wide range of targets, such as the ten digits, 0 to 9, or the twelve units of the clock face. More elaborate safeguards are described on p. 157. A rating table for the evaluation of scores obtained from standard ESP test-card runs is given on p. 191.

The DT Test. This technique for testing clairvoyance is the same as BT except for the fact that after the experimenter has shuffled and cut the pack, he places it face down and does not do anything more to it until the subject has completed the twenty-five calls. (The DT test may, of course, also be done in sections of five trials.) Provided the experimenter puts the pack of cards back in the box after the shuffling and before bringing it into the subject's range of vision, there is no need to use a screen in the DT test. The DT test also allows the subject to proceed at his own rate of speed.

Matching Techniques. These are clairvoyance tests in which the subject indicates his impression of a target card by matching it against one of a set of key cards lying in a row in front of him. Different degrees of precaution are allowable; for instance, as a very preliminary form of matching test, the five key cards are turned face up. The subject in this *open matching* test is handed the pack of cards already shuffled and it is kept in the inverted position while he distributes the cards from the top, laying them

Blind Matching. *Upper:* Subject sorting cards against concealed key cards
Lower: The check-up.

one by one face-down in piles opposite the key cards. He is of course trying to place each card of the pack against the key card it matches. It should be explained to him that he does not have to make the piles even, and that he should not fall into a rhythm or pattern. The subject should keep his eyes focused upon the key cards rather than upon the backs of the cards in his hands. At the end of the run the experimenter turns over each pile of cards, sorts out the hits, and adds up and records the score.

The *blind matching* test is a better controlled procedure. In this the five key cards, one of each symbol, are (unseen by the subject) put in opaque envelopes and the five envelopes, after being shuffled so that the order is not known, are laid out in a row on the table. The subject proceeds with the shuffled pack of cards held face down in the same way as in the open matching test. In this case he is matching the inverted card in the pack against the concealed card in the envelope, with no sensory contact with either of the two symbols he is trying to match against each other.

The *screened touch-matching* technique is the most widely used and most satisfactory matching test, but it requires a special screen (similar to that shown facing page 161). This type of screen (approximately 18″ high by 24″ in length) can, however, easily be improvised from a large carton; at the bottom an opening about $2^{1}/_{2}″$ high and from 12″ to 15″ in length is needed. The five key cards are laid in this opening so that they can be seen by the experimenter on one side of the screen and by the subject on the other. Another low screen about 3″ high should be set up on the experimenter's side, back a little from the main screen, to prevent the subject from getting any reflected image or a direct glimpse of the card through the opening. In this case the experimenter holds the pack of cards, which he has shuffled behind the screen. The subject is given a pencil or other pointer to use in indicating which one of the key cards he thinks will match the top card in the pack in the experimenter's hand. As soon as he sees the pointer over a key card the experimenter lays the top card of the pack (still inverted) down opposite that key, and the subject points to the next one, proceeding at his own rate of speed.

In preliminary tests it will satisfy many explorers merely to sort out in each pile the cards that match the key card and add up the total score for the run. As the instructions in the later section of this chapter will indicate (p. 159) there are many added pre-

cautions that may be taken step by step to rule out possibilities
of error of one kind or another. At a certain stage of advance the
experimenter will wish to record on conveniently prepared record
sheets the way the cards are distributed.

C. ESP Tests: 2. General Extrasensory Perception or GESP

The GESP test (or telepathy-card test) is a procedure suitable
for subjects who believe that for them psi operates best as telepathy. It is the BT technique with the difference that the experimenter or another person acting as sender looks at the card
during the trial (instead of keeping it face down). Even in the
most preliminary type of tests it is advisable to screen not only
the cards but the experimenter himself from the subject's view.
In an informal beginning the subject may be seated in a mirrorless
corner of the room with his back to the experimenter, but an
opaque screen sufficient to conceal the experimenter from view is
a better provision. It is still better to use two adjoining rooms
with the two participants on opposite sides of the door or wall.
Even if the testing is begun with both participants in the same
room the two-room arrangement is a desirable advance as soon as
success warrants a change.

It is necessary for the subject to be given only one trial for each
target card and for the experimenter to make no remark or indication of any kind once he has picked up the card for the next
trial. The subject is the one who should indicate (by a word or
a tap on the wall) when the next trial is to begin. While it is a
more careful procedure to have the subject silently record his own
responses (and without the experimenter being able to see the
record as the test proceeds) a beginning can safely be made in
which the subject merely calls his choice aloud and the experimenter keeps the record. (In such a case, it is better to leave the
card recording until after the run.) In more careful procedures
the subject records his calls and the experimenter records the
cards, both independently, and there are thus two separate records which at the end of the run the two can check together.
With this procedure, either with a good screen or with the two-
room arrangement, the experimenter may be reasonably sure he
is not allowing sensory cues to be given or recording errors to

occur. For the next stage of precaution he will want to consult the more crucial procedures on pp. 159–161.

D. ESP Test: 3. Precognition

A simple precognition test is needed to initiate subjects who have difficulty accepting the possibility that ESP may reach into the future. The subject may be instructed to predict (and record) what he thinks the order of a given pack of cards will be when it is next shuffled and cut. During the first stages the experimenter himself may do this shuffling and cutting. It is an advance on this method, then, to take the pack to another individual who does not know about the test and merely ask him to shuffle and cut the pack (always using a knife or thumbnail cut). Then with continued success the subject is encouraged to advance to a further precautionary stage, and at this point he may be instructed to put down in the call column a set of symbols which he anticipates will match the target symbols to be recorded in the adjoining column when the randomized target order has been selected. This target selection can be designated as taking place immediately after the run or at any time in the future the experimenter desires. Then, after the run or series of runs of subject's calls have been recorded, the following exploratory procedure would give a reasonably good assurance that only precognition could produce nonchance results.

Randomizing Procedure. The procedure should, of course, be worked out in advance and followed each time in a literal, routine way. A pair of dice is thrown twice and the faces recorded. One die is marked in advance as giving the left digit and the other the right. Then, using the local telephone directory, let the first pair of numbers indicate the page (between 11 and 66) and the second pair the number of names to count off before beginning on that page. Then, with the beginning point indicated, the rule would be to choose the second column of numbers from the right. Also, let it be agreed that numbers 1 and 6 will be circle, 2 and 7 cross, 3 and 8 waves, 4 and 9 square, 5 and 0 star. Then by going down the column and taking the first twenty-five numbers and converting them to symbols, the target order would be obtained for the

LIBRARY ST. MARY'S COLLEGE

first run. Going on to the next twenty-five would give the target order for the second run and so on.

This provides an easy method of testing for precognition without encumbering the experimenter with the complicated procedure required for a more crucial test as described on pp. 162–163 of this chapter.

E. PK Test: 1. With Face Targets

Possibly the most simple adequate test of PK is the method of throwing dice and using a selected face as target. For beginning subjects a pair of dice will serve better than a larger number. The dice need not be of the so-called "perfect" classification, although if obtainable they should at least be of the inlaid variety, which leaves no cavities where the spots are marked. It should be settled from the beginning that a fixed order of target faces will be followed, and we recommend the standard plan of beginning with one and following through in the regular sequence to six. The manner of throwing or releasing the dice is important, although it is less important if the subject is obviously a person unskilled in dice games. For an informal beginning the dice may be thrown from a cup or substitute container, but with smooth surfaces these are little better than hand throwing. Cups with properly roughened interior can be made, and as the exploring becomes more serious they should be introduced.

There is, however, no reason why the tests for PK should not from the beginning use a simple device for gravity action such as the following: A board one foot in width and three feet long is about all the equipment that is needed. With two nails driven in lightly a few inches apart at one end and a ruler laid across the nails, a shelf can be made for the dice as the board is inclined at the proper angle against the wall (let us say at about 45 degrees). The dice are laid on the ruler opposite pencil markings on the board. Then the subject can, when he is ready, simply lift the ruler and allow the dice to roll down the inclined board onto the surface prepared for them—either on the floor or, more conveniently, on a blanketed table top with side walls to retain the dice. Then, with the understanding that the dice are to be picked up as they fall and placed on the ruler with the same faces uppermost, the apparatus is ready. The surface of the board can be improved by the addition of a piece of rubber matting.

It is important to have a definite plan for the experiment. The standard run consists of twenty-four die throws. Two dice released twelve times make a run. It should be determined in advance how many runs will be done with the one-face before changing to the two-face, and so on. If a very short test session is desired, one run for each target face will be sufficient. Or the plan of the experiment may be laid down for six or twelve or more runs for a given face at one session and for the same number of runs on the other faces at succeeding sessions.

There are a few rules each experimenter will wish to follow. One is to avoid the mistake of starting with a lucky throw; this is done best by saying in advance when the next release is on the record. Again, every throw must be put on the record unless conditions specified in advance have interfered; for instance, if one die rolls off the table or lands in a cocked position against the sidewall, the trial should be repeated (that is, with both dice). For exploratory purposes the experimenter's record alone will be sufficient. It adds something to the accuracy of recording, however, for the experimenter quietly to name the faces as he records, unless by so doing he distracts the subject.

There are many varieties of PK tests possible with dice, and, of course, other objects too may be used, though they are less convenient. But the use of dice and the single target face are undoubtedly best for a beginning.

Table II (p. 192) indicates the significance of PK scores with die faces as targets. More advanced precautions are described in a later section (pp. 164–167).

F. PK Tests: 2. Placement Method

For the placement test of PK a more tightly constructed apparatus is needed, though it need not be an expensive one. Even for exploratory purposes the apparatus should be set upon a solid table and no one should be allowed to come into contact with the table or apparatus except to pick up the dice (or other objects) and return them to the release point. A blanketed table top with a fixed retaining wall is needed, and above it a release point and slope over which the dice are to roll. All this should be attached to the table or wall in such a way that the whole apparatus is a stable unit. The release point and slope should be so adjusted that the dice are, in falling, well distributed over the area of the table top. A midline should be marked off longitudinally, dividing the area into a left half and a right. If this dividing line is marked by a cord or wire drawn tight on the surface it will leave no doubt as to which side of the line a die is on when it falls on the line.

For preliminary exploration the dice may be released by the frictionless removal of a barrier such as the ruler described in the preceding method, freeing the dice to the pull of gravity. Or a trap can be operated by a string working through a fixed point and allowing only a uniform impulse (e.g., from the dropping of a weight in the same way each time) for pulling the string. It will be advisable, however, for the explorer to introduce at an early stage the smoother operation of an electrically-released trapdoor. This can be purchased all ready to be attached to the apparatus. It should be operated by a pushbutton on a cord held without tension so that the apparatus can be in no way mechanically influenced by the subject's release of the dice. The starting box should be built so that the dice all have to slide out through the same V-shaped trough when the trapdoor at the lower end is opened.

When the apparatus is ready and the subject is prepared for the task, he should be consulted (after preliminary trials) as to how many dice he would like to release at a time. In this type of test it is probably better to use more than two, though perhaps not more than ten. When that point is settled and the extent of the experiment decided, five releases should be made for the left side and then five for the right. This may be followed by a return to the left unless the experimenter has some reason for a different order of scheduling. The task of the subject is, of course, to try to exert a direct mental influence upon the fall of the cubes so as to make them roll into the target section. The scoring in a placement test is based on the difference of the total successes between the two sides, target and nontarget. Accordingly, the left and right side must be alternated as target in some regular way and kept entirely even.   The general practice has been to use one side as target for 5 times and then an equal number for the other side.

While cubes have been most often used, other objects may be introduced, especially spherical objects; but the more successful work has been done thus far with cubes.

Placement test of psychokinesis (PK).

The expectation, if the table and apparatus were perfectly balanced, would be 50 per cent on the target side by chance alone, but because of the many irregularities to be expected the only reliable measure would be the difference between the target side (which was equally represented by the left and the right) and the nontarget side.   These should on the theory of chance be equal. By turning to Table III on page 193, results from placement tests may be evaluated.   Again, in a later section, the more advanced precautions are to be found (pp. 164–167).

III. Conclusive Test Methods

A. General Viewpoint

Whereas the methods of the preceding section were cast on a level aimed only to enable the explorer to satisfy himself as to his findings, in the present section methods are added that, accompanied by significant results, will allow definite conclusions to be drawn with all reasonable alternatives eliminated. The scope included in these procedures covers the range of errors such as sensory cues, recording and checking errors, evaluative and interpretative mistakes on the part of research workers plus even the possibilities of deceptive practice on the part of the subjects. This coverage will not be extended to the delicate question of probity in the investigators themselves. In scientific research such questions are answered in due time by independent confirmation of the original findings.

Advance Record of Design. A proposed experiment should be recorded fully and clearly enough so that all the main features are decided from the start. Among these is the research question or questions to be answered, the method to be followed, the number of trials to be made, the subjects to be used, the test conditions, and the evaluative procedures to be applied to the data. These are best worked out either on the basis of previous experiments or with the help of the pilot test method described in Chapter 2. The design of the experiment should be such that if significant results are obtained only one conclusion can properly be drawn regarding each question raised.

Two-experimenter Plan. Both in ESP and PK tests it is difficult to conduct conclusive experiments without two research workers, either with both actively engaged in the testing or at least with one actively at work and another conveniently available in the background. The two-experimenter plan calls for the sharing of the essential responsibility for test accuracy in such a way that errors by one experimenter alone could not possibly produce significant results. It should be so that nothing short of a deliberate joint effort on the part of both experimenters could allow or produce errors to affect the results in a significant direction and degree. If, for example, there are records of cards and of calls to be made, each experimenter can be made responsible for one of these; and by making duplicates and exchanging them, each will have an independent set of the whole record for individual checking and evaluation.

Target Order. For general purposes the methodical shuffling of cards with a minimum of four dovetail shuffles and a knife cut sufficiently approximates a random distribution for ESP test purposes. For certain experiments the pack of cards (if cards are to be used) can be made up on the basis of random number tables,* letting certain numbers represent specific symbols. Any fixed code would do, but the one given on p. 151 has been adopted as standard in the Parapsychology Laboratory; it is a great convenience in rechecking data if a uniform code is used. In other experiments the cards themselves are not needed, and a recorded target order, whether of the standard ESP symbols or some other set of targets, can be taken from random number tables in the same way.

B. ESP Tests: 1. Clairvoyance

The BT Test. Only a few additions to the exploratory BT test are needed to make it conclusive. If the subject is asked to record his own calls, the record should be made in duplicate by the use of a carbon sheet. The screen used to keep the cards invisible to the subject should be large enough to screen his recording from the view of the experimenter on the opposite side. At the end of the run the experimenter, too, makes his card record in duplicate and before any checking is done the subject and experimenter both turn copies of their records over to the second experimenter. (The latter is either in the room or nearby. Provision can even be made for the sealing and mailing of these records to the second experimenter or for their deposit in locked boxes he may provide for the purpose, but it is better to have the second experimenter on the scene if possible.)

---

* A suitable table is that of Kendall and Smith, *Tables of Random Sampling Numbers,* published by Cambridge University Press and priced at five shillings ($0.70).

If the subject is, for some reason, not asked to record his own calls, the second experimenter should write them. If all the participants of the test are in the same room and the subject makes his responses orally, it is necessary that the card order have been recorded in advance. The conclusive BT test can be carried out best with the use of different rooms and a signaling system. Adjoining rooms will provide sufficient safeguards, since the experimenter does not look at the faces of the cards. The two experimenters, after checking the records independently, should enter all scores in a permanent notebook and should carry out all analyses and computations independently as well.

The DT Test. A conclusive form of this test can be taken over from the instructions just given for the BT method. The packs of cards (or columns of target symbols will do as well) should be prepared outside of the room in which the subject is being tested and they should be properly enclosed before being brought into the experimental room. Since the test is to be a clairvoyance test, the experimenter using a target pack or column of symbols must not know the order. One experimenter in the room is enough, and it is better for the psychological effect not to have idle observers sitting around during the test. If the second experimenter prepared and recorded the targets in an adjoining room, he should remain there with duplicate records of the targets in his possession. Then either the subject or the first experimenter (whichever one does the recording of the subject's calls) can conveniently turn over to him the carbon of the subject's call record. Thus each experimenter will have an independent set of both calls and cards and separate score records of the entire experiment. Again, independent checking and evaluation should be carried through.

The DT method with slight modifications lends itself well to correspondence tests. (The first experimenter makes copies of the target records, or duplicate records of the cards if cards are to be sent, before sending them out.) Either the pack of cards or the original sheet of target symbols is sealed with special care and sent by this experimenter to the local representative (let us say a teacher) who is to collect the subject's call records. The envelopes sent to this representative for the return of the subject's call records is addressed to the other experimenter, who shall also receive the unopened packs or target sheets. Duplicates of the subject's call records are, on receipt by the second experimenter, turned over at once to the first, leaving each experimenter with a set of the target and call records. The local representative should be instructed not to allow the sealed targets out of her sight during the test performance.

Matching Techniques. For a conclusive test of *blind matching* one experimenter prepares the key cards, preferably enclosing them in opaque envelopes. The other experimenter, who is to remain present throughout the test, presents the subject with the shuffled and cut pack of cards, and the latter then proceeds to distribute these one by one opposite the key cards, keeping them inverted throughout. At the end of the run the experimenter turns over the piles of target cards and records them. He takes the carbon of this record to the second experimenter (who may be waiting in an adjoining room) and receives from him a copy of the order of the key cards. Each experimenter can thus check on the number of successes at his convenience and keep his own permanent record of the scores. The subject can also be shown the key cards and see the number of hits made.

The screened touch-matching test proceeds in much the same way in its more conclusive form. The first experimenter, who handles the pack of cards on the opposite side of the screen from the subject, should not be allowed to see the order of the key cards; these are clipped or otherwise attached to the subject's side of the screen. The arrangement of the key cards is under the care of the second experimenter who reshuffles their order before each run and then records the key card order in duplicate (*in reverse,* as they would appear from the second experimenter's side of the screen) before the run is completed. At the end of the run the first experimenter turns over the piles of target cards and records them in duplicate. After exchanging carbons with the other experimenter, the screen may be laid down and the subject allowed to do his own checking. Each of the two experimenters has a complete set of records for keeping independent scores.

C. ESP Tests: 2. GESP

In all GESP tests for conclusive work the target order needs to be recorded in advance and the record as well as the cards, of

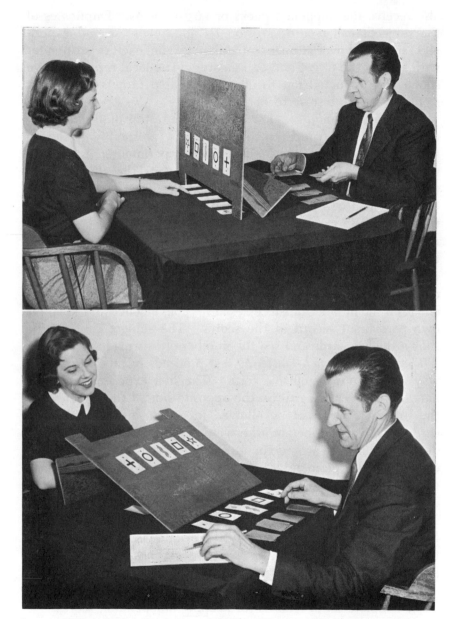

Screened Touch-Matching test of ESP. *Upper:* The test in progress.
Lower: The check-up.

course, carefully guarded. In this, as in other points of precaution, if one of the experimenters is to act as agent or sender, a simpler arrangement is possible. But if *both* sender and receiver are "subjects" and are to be considered independent of the experimental team, the possibility of a wide range of sensory means of communication exists and would have to be eliminated by providing adequate conditions. It is difficult to do this with short distances between the two participants because of the possibility of utilizing (for example) tiny concealed electronic devices for signaling. If, however, one of the experimenters serves as sender (or receiver) the use of adjoining rooms with closed doors will be sufficient safeguard against sensory cues. The necessary signaling should in all cases come from the subject or receiver who indicates when he is ready for the next trial. No signaling or communication from the sender is allowable after the run has begun.

The receiver may prefer to record his own calls and may do better in isolation. Or the second experimenter may record the subject's calls. In the event he is not needed as recorder, the second experimenter should remain in such a location (e.g., in an intermediate room or hallway) that he can at all times be sure the receiver is not out of position. Before the test the target series should have been recorded in duplicate and a copy should be in the possession of each experimenter. Following the completion of the subject's record in duplicate, these two copies are also divided between the two experimenters. Again the complete record is held by each, and the independent handling of the data from that point on is an insurance against errors of importance.

The possibilities of subject trickery are so great and varied that in a GESP test involving a sender and receiver who are not a part of the experimental team, and who may have developed a signalling system, a special research design would be needed. It would not be possible to lay down in advance a set of rules that could apply to all possibilities in so uncertain a situation. But from the research point of view it would be a situation to be avoided, if possible, by using another type of ESP test.

D. ESP Test: 3. Precognition

Tests for precognition can easily be guarded against the ordinary types of error. When the subject's record sheets are completed in duplicate, these are held by one experimenter until the target records are made out by the other. When these are prepared the two experimenters exchange copies and the experiment is at all times on a safe basis of independent checking, computation, and score filing.

The main difficulty of finding a conclusive test of precognition has been the problem of making sure of a truly random selection of targets. The following procedure may, we believe, be followed with the confidence that no alternative known to science today offers a serious challenge to the method. The procedure should be in the hands of a second experimenter who has not thus far seen the subject's record sheets. The first experimenter, who has them in his possession, may be present as a witness or an assistant may be substituted as an observer during the various steps in the procedure.

Three special ten-faced dice are needed as well as a calculating machine. The experimenter throws the three dice, each of which is distinguishable by some mark or color. The faces turned up are recorded in the same order each time—for example: red, white, blue. The three dice are thrown four times, thus giving four three-digit numbers. These numbers are then multiplied together in a calculating machine. The first ten digits of the product, counting from the right, are multiplied by a number consisting of the same digits read in reverse order. The machine is then used to extract the square root of the ten left-hand digits of this product. The square root is recorded in duplicate and kept by both experimenters.

The square root is used to pick a starting place in a random number table. For the Kendall and Smith table, for example, the last two digits on the right indicate which of the 100 thousand-digit groups to take; the fifth, fourth, and third digits are divided by 40, the number of columns on the page, and the remainder taken to indicate the column; and the seventh and sixth digits are divided by 25, the number of digits in the column, and the remainder taken to indicate the digit in the column to be used for the first target. This is determined by the prearranged (and recorded) number-symbol code. For the other targets the numbers from the table should be read in the order suggested by the authors of the random number table (or by a system recorded at the start) until a full set of targets is made up.

Simplifications of this complex procedure might be worked out that would be satisfactory. The essential point is to have rigid rules that still allow for such variations as are introduced by the throw of the dice. Then, to eliminate the possible alternative of psychokinesis, it is necessary to have a complicated mechanical calculation that is beyond the possibility of the human mind. (Computations by means of logarithm and root tables might be substituted for the use of the machine if one is not available. And cutting three decks of number cards would do instead of the dice if they are hard to locate.) It may be important not to burden the subject with a full explanation of how the targets will be selected but to tell him only that they will be random targets to be found at a later time. But if he is told that the target series will be recorded in a column adjoining the call record or will be located in some other specific place at a given time, the experimental operation should (at least until we know more about the ability) conform to this understanding.

While the mere technical requirements for a conclusive test of precognition are high, in striving to achieve them the experimenter must not neglect the even more important *psychological* requirements. Unless the subject is properly prepared for a test in precognition, the most careful attention to procedural details is so much wasted effort. The research done heretofore indicates that the motivation required for a successful precognition test may be much more difficult to bring about than that for ordinary ESP. An experimenter should tackle the precognition problem only if he appreciates this fact and still feels that the challenge and importance of this research area make it *the one* into which he wants to venture. At the present stage of the research, it is desirable always to incorporate into the experiment at least a small section of simple clairvoyance tests for purposes of comparison with the results of the precognition trials.

E. PK Test Procedures

Both in the use of faces as targets and in placement methods conclusive experiments require a two-experimenter plan unless a system of automatic counting or recording can be provided. Even in that case, an independent check on the apparatus would be necessary. In any event, since the apparatus necessary for such a system is elaborate, we will describe the methods without assuming that it will be available.

The point of greatest emphasis in making the PK test crucial will be in the accuracy of recording. The other points to be watched can be handled more easily. Whenever recording depends upon the human observer alone (that is, is nonphotographic or nonmechanical) two independent recorders are needed for conclusive tests based on the standard measures of scoring effects. This applies equally well both to the target face and to the placement methods.

Again, as in exploratory testing, it is not necessary to be concerned with perfection, either in the dice (or other objects used) or in the apparatus used. Adequate control over possible imperfections must be included in the design of the test. It is a more important point that if there is to be any human contact with the dice during the test, they be handled only by the experimenters and not by the subjects. The possibility would otherwise have to be recognized that in the target-face tests the subject, in picking up the dice, might use a trick (e.g., substituting loaded dice by slight of hand) borrowed from the gambling arts.

To eliminate the alternative of precognition, remote though it is as a possibility, the strict adherence to a standard sequence of target order will be necessary unless some other provision is made for this requirement. (Other methods have been discussed in Chapter 3.)

In the activation of the dice it is highly advantageous, if not, indeed, necessary to use a mechanical method of release even with target-face experiments. A method permitting the dice to fall or tumble under the force of gravity combines the advantages of safety and simplicity. In tests with faces as targets, rotating (motor-driven) transparent cages can be used to good advantage as they make it unnecessary for the dice to be handled by anyone during the experiment.   If a stationary release point is used and if a proper table is constructed, the same apparatus can be used for either face or place as targets.   It should have an electrically-operated release box and the latter should be firmly attached to the table together with a connecting incline of proper angle for the greatest activation of the dice.   The procedure must include

PK test for target face with machine-thrown dice.

adequate safeguards against altering the position of or jarring the apparatus or otherwise physically influencing the dice at the time of release, so as to affect the results in any way.   The subject should always be in the same position during the test though he may be encouraged to choose at the start the place that he finds most satisfactory.

The release box should be constructed with a V-shaped bottom, long enough to hold the objects in a single row.   This will give a uniform release direction to all objects when the trapdoor is opened, which is especially important in a placement test.   Unless the design of the experiment calls for a different plan the dice in a test for target face may be dropped into the release box in a random fashion. Shaking in cupped hands (picking up in a cup or using a loading chute) will insure this as the dice are dropped in the box.

Strict rules should be laid down in advance concerning doubtful cases of cocked dice or dice that fall from the table or lodge in the apparatus. Each incomplete trial should be left unrecorded and repeated in full. Every possible provision should be made to eliminate cases where judgment is required to interpret the results. If judgment is ever necessary, it must always be made on the conservative side; that is, favoring the chance hypothesis.

With nothing left to consider but the place or face of the dice, the experimenters can give full attention to the psychological needs of the subject, which, in a more highly controlled experiment, are greater than in a simpler test. The presence of a second record-taker is likely to be a handicap to the subject unless this observer can keep himself quietly inconspicuous, making notations and preparing record sheets. The first experimenter should handle the dice (if necessary) as well as keep his own record of all dice (i.e., faces or positions). While both observers must be in a position to see the dice themselves, their records should generally not be visible to the other recorder.

All these precautions, however fully thought out and seriously taken by the experimenters themselves, need to be kept effectively in the background so far as the subject is concerned. As has been stated repeatedly, the test is not a psi test in reality unless the psychological conditions are such as to allow psi to function. A too officious attention to the details of safeguarding can be distracting to most subjects.

Both general types of PK tests lend themselves easily to a great variety of adaptations. The reseach worker is likely to think of interesting variations that have special appeal for him or perhaps for a particular subject. Such departures are highly desirable when taken at the proper stage. Good scientific procedure calls for making such a departure only after successful experience with the standard lines of investigation. Even then the inclusion of a section based on standard methods right along with each new adaptation tried is a wise and proper course to follow. The results are bound to be more meaningful and conclusive with this more comparative basis for interpretation. Always, of course, it is well to keep in mind the advantages of the pilot-test method in projecting new programs of research. This guarded approach will help the experimenter to decide how long the test series should be, which analyses would be best, and whether the project is generally feasible.

IV. Summarizing Comments

Emphasis is needed on a few main considerations. Each worker will, in his own experience, come upon these points, but much time can be saved if he can take them under consideration early.

First, let us underscore the importance of a worker's recognizing the stage at which he is engaged. If he is *beginning* an inquiry he should not allow himself to be burdened with the heavy considerations of *conclusive* testing. The scout would be unduly handicapped by such heavy equipment. The freedom to search quickly, lightly, and over a wider range is precious to the early explorer. It is equally important, of course, once an explorer finds himself reasonably satisfied about something he thinks important, that he should advance to the methods of making more certain for himself and for his fellow scientists. This justifies and even urgently requires the more crucial types of testing such as those described in the section just preceding.

Second, we could not urge too strongly the importance of the subjective conditions needed for such experiments as these methods are meant to serve. The objective routines are by far the easier part to handle, and the less important as well. They are quite useless and even a waste of time unless the atmosphere of the test situation is adequately taken into account. The mental state of the subject in approaching and taking part in the test is a proper first consideration, then, in any psi experiment. The objective methods we have been describing are merely the secondary equipment, the machinery necessary to the operation.

Third, it should be recognized that not many of the most important researches in parapsychology were done with a very clear concept of rule and method in mind. Pioneer workers are likely to be rule makers and even rule breakers rather than rule followers. This we anticipate will continue to be the case. The value of these methods, then, as formulated, is to provide an advantageous start for those who wish to begin as far up toward the front as possible, for most of whom psi testing must remain a matter incidental to other professional practice and work. Those who will be drawn further into the depth of parapsychological investigation as a professional career will, in due time, take these more basic procedures as points of departure for such advances as their own fresh inquiries will demand. Yet even for them the benefits of already prepared basic methods will neither be lost nor forgotten.

Fourth, in emphasizing the need for certain standardized tests we do *not* (as we have said) mean to discourage innovations as far as these prove interesting and useful. The point that most needs emphasizing for the research worker in parapsychology is the importance of giving free rein to his own inventive genius in the development of new and perhaps better devices of inquiry. Perhaps most important of all in this connection is the psychological need of the experimenter himself to experience the enjoyment of breaking new ground. In the same breath, then, that the importance of first becoming acquainted with standard, established procedure is emphasized, can be stressed with equal force the need to advance beyond mere repetition. The experimenter needs to move ahead one step at a time, all the while introducing fresh novelty into every progressive effort.

Additional Reading

KAHN, S. D.: Studies in extrasensory perception. *Proc. Am. Soc. Psychical Res.*, 25:1–48, 1952.

RHINE, J. B.: Requirements and suggestions for an ESP test machine. *J. Parapsychol.*, 3:3–10, 1939.

SCHERER, W.: Spontaneity as a factor in ESP. *J. Parapsychol.*, 12:126–147, 1948.

STUART, C. E., and PRATT, J. G.: *A Handbook for Testing Extrasensory Perception.* New York, Farrar and Rhinehart, 1937.

TYRRELL, G. N. M.: The Tyrrell apparatus for testing extrasensory perception. *J. Parapsychol.*, 2:107–118, 1938.

WEBSTER, D. D.: An automatic testing and recording device for experiments in extrasensory perception. *J. Parapsychol.*, 13:107–117, 1949.

WEST, D. J.: *Tests for Extrasensory Perception: An Introductory Guide.* London, Society for Psychical Research, 1954.

Chapter 9

Statistical Methods

I. Introduction

T HE RATING tables (pp. 191–193) giving an approximate evaluation of psi test results have already been mentioned. These obvi-
ate the necessity of making statistical calculations. The present
chapter will describe, for the benefit of those who may wish to
know how to make a more exact evaluation of their results, the
statistical methods most widely used in parapsychology.

The methods needed to evaluate results from the tests explained
in the preceding chapter will be described in some detail. Other
statistical methods have also been used in parapsychology, and
the more important of these will be mentioned, with references to
the literature in which full descriptions may be found. The statistical methods are considered here solely from the point of view of
their application; that is, no effort will be made to examine the
theory or give the derivation of any of the procedures. In the
main the methods are well-known procedures which are discussed
in the statistical textbooks.* In some instances, however, experimenters in parapsychology have raised questions in connection
with test results that could not be evaluated by the available
methods. These questions have led to advances in statistics to
provide the new methods required.

A. Some General Requirements

A statistical test of significance is simply a means of evaluating
a result in relation to what might be expected on a purely chance
basis. For the evaluation to serve its purpose, it is of the greatest
importance to make sure that no nonchance factors are allowed

---

* See the list at the end of this chapter.

to enter the situation except the one which the test is designed to measure (for example, ESP). There must be no selection nor omission of trials in a manner that could conceivably affect the final results. The length of the series to be done should be stated in advance to avoid the risk of simply picking a favorable stopping point. The targets must provide the same probability or range of choice on each trial and their order must be random or sufficiently close to a random one to meet this basic assumption of statistical analysis. Only one call may be allowed for an ESP trial, and only one die-throw for a PK trial.

The analysis to be used should be decided upon before the test is done, though this question is not likely to trouble the beginning experimenter who has a limited choice of statistical methods. In particular, the use of a number of evaluations upon the same data in a search for one that seems to give significant results is rarely profitable. Such selection of the best analysis after the data have been examined is no more legitimate than the selection of good test results. Of course, it is permissible in some instances to plan at the outset to evaluate results in two or more designated ways, such as checking direct target scoring and forward and backward displacement. If this is done, an appropriate correction must be made in the probability figure given by the most significant evaluation, such as multiplying the P-value by the number of analyses made. The methods described in this chapter for the evaluation of direct-target scores apply also to displacement scores, but it is necessary to take account of the exact number of "trials" (call-card comparisons) involved when checking displacement (e.g., there are only 24 "trials" involved when each call is checked against the target one position ahead in the run).

If the closed pack (equal numbers of each type of symbol) is used in an ESP test the subject may not be told whether he is right or wrong on each trial unless the pack is to be reshuffled before the test proceeds; otherwise the subject gains a certain unallowable advantage from his knowledge of what symbols have already been used in the pack as he can infer which ones are left and thus improve his chances.

The subject may be permitted to do trials "off the record" as a means of building up his confidence, but the experimenter who

uses this device must make sure that it is explicitly stated before
the trial is made when it is not to be counted and also when the
next trial is to be the first one of the "on the record" series.

B. Statistical Tables

Statistical evaluations are often made more quickly and easily
by the use of tables which list some of the necessary values, already worked out for the cases most frequently required. A
number of such tables applying to the methods described in this
chapter are given at the back of the book. Some of the tables
apply to the results of specific test procedures; their use will be
explained and references made to them at appropriate points in
the descriptions of the statistical methods. One table that is basic
to a number of statistical methods is that by which the "critical
ratio" (CR) associated with a test result may be translated into a
probability of occurrence on a chance basis. Such a probability
value (P) is the objective of every statistical analysis, and if P is
sufficiently small the "chance" explanation becomes unreasonable
and the evaluation is said to be statistically significant.* The
criterion of significance, an arbitrarily selected value which P must
not exceed if the chance hypothesis is to be rejected, may be taken
as .01 for a result interpreted in terms of the *amount of the deviation from the chance average without regard to the sign or direction of the deviation.* The use of a criterion of significance is discussed more fully later in the chapter.

No effort will be made to define every statistical term used in the
text. A number of definitions are given in the glossary.

II. *Evaluation of a Total Score*

A. ESP Card Test

Given: an ESP series of 25 runs (625 trials) with a total score
of 160 hits. What is the statistical significance of this result?

The most likely chance score, or *mean chance expectation*

---

* For example, if a P-value of .01 is obtained, this means that in an experiment
such as the one under consideration a result, considered solely in terms of random
variation of scores, would differ from the expected chance average by as much as
the one obtained an average of only 1 time in 100 repetitions of the series.

(MCE), for a series of this length is $1/5 \times 625 = 125$ hits. Expressed in general terms, $MCE = np$, where n is the number of trials and p is the probability of a hit on each one.

The deviation (Dev.) is $160 - 125 = +35$. The deviation is positive in sign if the observed score is greater than MCE, and negative when the observed score is less than MCE. The formula, $Dev. = Observed\ Score - MCE$, gives the deviation with its correct sign.

The standard deviation is $2\sqrt{\text{no. of runs}} = 2\sqrt{25} = 10$. This is a convenient computation formula which applies to standard ESP runs of 25 trials. It is derived from the general formula for the variance of the binomial distribution: $Var. = npq$. where n and p are as already defined, and $q = 1 - p$, or the probability of scoring a miss on any given call. The standard deviation is the square root of the variance, or $\sqrt{npq}$. For the 625-trial series this becomes $\sqrt{625 \times 1/5 \times 4/5}$, which reduces to $2\sqrt{\text{no. of runs}}$.

The *critical ratio* (CR) is the deviation divided by the standard deviation, or in the present case, $+35/10 = +3.5$.

The *probability* (P) is found by looking up the CR in a table which shows areas under the normal curve in relation to CR values. A table for the conversion of CR values to P values is given on page 197. From this it may be seen that the P value associated with a CR of 3.5 is .0005. This means that only about 5 times in 10,000 would a score in a 25-run series deviate from MCE by as much as the observed score through mere chance coincidence. In other words, the fact that the score does not fall *between* 90 and 160 is very unlikely—so unlikely that the chance hypothesis is not a reasonable explanation of the results. The score of 160 hits on 25 runs is therefore statistically significant.

Since the above evaluation is based upon the *amount* of the deviation without regard to its direction from MCE, the level of statistical significance would be the same for a total score of 90 on 25 runs, or a negative deviation of 35 hits. Because of the psi-missing effect, the general practice has become one of interpreting CR's in this manner that allows for the occurrence of either positive or negative deviations. This is done in the CR table given on page 197.

A table of SD values for ESP tests is given on page 194.

B. PK Test for Target Faces

Suppose a PK test for target faces consisting of 20 runs (480 die throws) has been completed with a total of 112 hits. What is the probability value for this score? Proceed in a manner similar to the one described for the ESP series above.

$$MCE = 1/6 \times 480 = 80 \text{ hits.}$$
$$Dev. = 112 - 80 = +32.$$
$$SD = \sqrt{npq} = \sqrt{480 \times 1/6 \times 5/6} = 8.17.$$

(For computational purposes, it can be shown that for the PK run of 24 dice throws $SD = 1.826 \sqrt{\text{no. of runs.}}$)

$$CR = +32/8.17 = 3.9.$$
$$P = .0001.$$

This means that a deviation as large as the one observed, or larger, in either direction from MCE would be expected to occur on the average only one time in 10,000 such series solely on the basis of chance variation in scores. Since the P value is below the .01 criterion of significance, the chance hypothesis may be rejected as an adequate explanation of this PK result.

A table of SD values for PK tests for target faces is given on page 195.

C. PK Placement Test

Suppose that a placement test has been completed which consists of 600 trials, 300 for each target area, and a total of 268 dice landed on the target side. To find the significance of this score, proceed as follows:

$$MCE = 1/2 \times 600 = 300$$
$$Dev. = 268 - 300 = -32$$
$$SD = \sqrt{600 \times 1/2 \times 1/2} = \sqrt{150} = 12.25$$
$$CR = -32/12.25 = -2.6$$
$$P = .01$$

The result is therefore statistically significant, though more of the dice came to rest on the side opposite to that which the subject was concentrating upon as the target.

A table of SD values for placement tests is given on page 196.

III. Evaluation of a Difference Between the Scores of Two Series

One question that may be raised in comparing the results obtained under two test conditions is whether the difference in scoring rate provides evidence for the operation of the psi process under investigation. From this point of view the two different test conditions may have been introduced as a psychological device to provide a more favorable situation for psi. For example, the experimenter may try to motivate the subject more strongly by challenging him to score *above* MCE and *below* MCE on alternate runs, and the plan of the experiment might provide for evaluating the difference between the high- and low-aim results as an indication that ESP was operating. Or again, a group of subjects might be separated into "sheep" and "goats" and the difference in scoring rate evaluated as a means of deciding whether ESP was demonstrated within the data as a whole. The following tests of significance for group differences apply, in a strict sense, only for this limited purpose of finding out if the chance hypothesis may be rejected.

A. Difference Between Two Groups of Equal Size

The procedure in this case is closely similar to that used in evaluating the total score of a single group of trials. Add the number of trials in the two equal groups and treat this as if it were the total number of trials of a *single* group. Take the difference between the total scores of the two groups and treat this difference as if it were the deviation from MCE of this "single" group. Proceed to evaluate the significance of the "total trials" and "deviation" in the appropriate manner as already described in the preceding section. As an illustration, consider the following example.

Assume that a subject did ordinary screened BT runs alternately with runs based on individual target cards sealed in opaque envelopes. According to the experimental plan, 50 runs were completed under each condition and the BT total score was 340 hits while that on the sealed targets (as checked at the end of the series) was 260 hits.

The total number of runs under both conditions is 100, and the difference between the two scores is 80. From this point onward the evaluation of the difference is parallel to the evaluation of the total score for the 25-run ESP series described in the preceding section. Therefore, the $CR_{diff.} = 4.0$ and $P = .00006$.

The difference between the scores obtained under the two conditions is therefore highly significant.

With equal groups in PK tests, whether for target faces or for placement, the method for evaluating the difference would proceed along comparable lines.

B. Difference Between Two Unequal Groups of Trials

When the number of trials done under the two conditions is not the same, it is obviously not possible merely to test the difference between the total scores of the two groups. It is necessary, therefore, to get the average rate of scoring within each group and to make a statistical test of the difference in averages. Since runs of 25 trials in ESP tests and of 24 trials in PK tests for target face have become standard, it is convenient to work with average run scores as the basis of the evaluation. If either group contains fewer than 30 runs, the t test (see p. 180) should be used as a statistical procedure applicable to small samples.

Assume that under Condition A 40 ESP runs yielded a total score of 275 hits and that under Condition B 60 ESP runs gave a total score of 305 hits. What is the significance of the difference between the results for Condition A and Condition B?

The average scoring rate of the A group is $275/40 = 6.875$ hits per run.

The average of the B group is $305/60 = 5.083$ hits per run.

The difference between run averages is therefore 1.792.

The standard deviation of this difference is given by the formula: $SD_{diff} = (SD \text{ of } 1 \text{ run}) \sqrt{1/R_1 + 1/R_2}$, where R_1 is the number of runs done under Condition A and R_2 is the number of runs done under Condition B. In the present instance, $SD_{diff} = 2\sqrt{1/40 + 1/60} = .408$.

The $CR_{diff} = 1.792/.408 = 4.4$

$P = .00001$. The difference between the two groups is therefore highly significant.

The same general procedure is followed in working out the difference between two unequal groups for PK target face results.

The standard deviation for 1 run of PK, however, is 1.826, and this value must be used in place of the standard deviation of 2 applied above as the appropriate one for the ESP run.

It is obvious that the evaluation of the difference between equal groups is more simple to do. An experimenter needs only to plan his research with equal groups in order to take advantage of the easier calculation.

A more advanced use of different test conditions than that of simply looking for further evidence of the occurrence of psi enters at a more advanced stage of the research. This is when the experimenter is no longer interested in simply proving the occurrence of ESP, precognition, or PK, but wants to discover something about the nature of psi processes. For a conclusive experiment at this stage, it is necessary to use a test of significance which assumes that psi may be present in the results, but to an unknown degree. The test uses the data themselves as a basis for estimating whether the ESP effect, say, was stronger under one or another test condition. The procedure most commonly used for this purpose is Student's *t* test which is described in general terms on page 180 and which is explained in more detail in the statistical texts listed at the end of this chapter.

IV. Some Uses of the Chi-Square Test

The chi-square test, like those based upon the critical ratio, provides a means of testing certain aspects of the data in terms of a theoretical chance distribution which has been established in mathematical statistics. Like any other statistical test, the chi-square analysis depends upon certain assumptions which must be satisfied to a reasonably close degree by the data to be analyzed. Two of the main assumptions are, first, that the probability of a success on each observation is the same for all the data and, secondly, that what happens on each trial is statistically independent of what happens on any of the other trials. These conditions are sufficiently well realized in most ESP and PK experiments to justify the use of a chi-square analysis, and a chi-square test sometimes contributes valuable information which is not furnished by other statistical analyses. Three applications of the chi-square analysis will be illustrated here.

A. Contingency Test Applied to ESP Data

A so-called five-by-five contingency table of ESP results shows the frequency with which each ESP call symbol was associated with the five different card symbols. Such a 25-cell table gives a more detailed picture of what occurred in the test than is obtained from the total score alone. An explanation of the chi-square test applied to a five-by-five table of ESP results is given in Appendix 5 of the book *Extrasensory Perception After Sixty Years*.[1] The investigator who wishes to use this method is referred to that source, or a discussion of it may be found in one of the standard textbooks on statistical methods.

B. Test of the Relationship Between Psi and Another Psychological Attribute

Investigators have been interested, for example, in whether ESP performance is related to the subject's attitude of belief or disbelief in ESP. For a valid test of such a relationship it is neces-

	Attitudes		
	Belief (Sheep)	Disbelief (Goats)	
Above MCE	(a) 27	(b) 12	(a+b) 39
At or Below MCE	(c) 9	(d) 23	(c+d) 32
	(a+c) 36	(b+d) 35	(a+b+c+d) 71

sary to take the individual subject as the unit of observation, and not the single ESP trial as has been done in the analyses considered up to this point.

Suppose that each of 71 subjects has taken an ESP test of 5 runs. Suppose also that each subject rated himself as a sheep (one who accepts the possibility of ESP) or a goat (one who rejects the possibility). Each subject is then tabulated according to whether he falls within the sheep or the goat category, and is further classified at the same time according to whether his ESP score was *above* MCE on the one hand, or was *at* or *below* MCE on the other hand. Suppose that this tabulation gives the distribution of subjects shown in the two-by-two table on the preceding page.

Such a table can be subjected to a chi-square test. With a calculating machine, the most convenient formula is as follows:

$$X^2 = \frac{(ad-bc)^2 \ (a+b+c+d)}{(a+b)(c+d)(a+c)(b+d)}$$

This chi square has one degree of freedom, and its square root is equivalent to a critical ratio.

In the above table, $X^2 = 11.88$ and $P = .0006$, and the result is therefore significant.[*] If the conditions of the test were sufficient to exclude other counterhypotheses, the conclusion could be drawn that a positive relationship exists between ESP scoring and belief in ESP.

C. Combination of Critical Ratios

Reversal of a relationship expressed a few lines above leads to the statement: the square of a CR is equivalent to X^2 with one degree of freedom. This fact, coupled with the further fact that chi squares may be added (and their degress of freedom added) to obtain larger values of X^2, provides a convenient way of making a joint evaluation of the CR's from two or more series of independent tests. The CR's are squared and added to get a X^2 value with as many degrees of freedom as the number of CR's used. This value of X^2 is looked up in a table of the chi-square distribution, where the P value may be read in the column for

---

[*] For a more accurate estimate of the probability in evaluations that come out near the criterion of significance, Yates' correction for discontinuity should be made in obtaining X^2 for tables having the observed value of any cell between 5 and 10. This consists of adding .5 to the smallest cell value and adjusting the other three cells to keep the marginal totals unchanged.

the correct number of degrees of freedom. This P value represents the significance of the results of the combined series. While it may be worth while in an exploratory investigation to combine CR's in this way as an afterthought, for a conclusive experiment it would be necessary to state in the plan the extent to which this test would be used as a basis of estimating the overall significance of the results.

V. *Other Methods of Statistical Evaluation*

A. General Methods

Within the limited scope of the present book, we can only call attention to other analyses which have been useful in parapsychological investigation. Some of these may assume a relatively more important position as the research advances.

The *correlation method* provides a means of finding out whether two functions that are measured tend to vary consistently, one in relation to the other. The *regression coefficient* is used for the same general purpose.

Student's t *test* is a means of estimating the significance of a total score or of a difference between two distributions. It does not depend upon a theoretical background distribution of the data, but uses statistical parameters of the distribution obtained from the observed data themselves. The most basic assumption of the t test is that the observed data are a random sample from a normally distributed population.

Analysis of variance is a statistical method by which a number of conceivable factors which might have influenced the results can be studied simultaneously on the basis of a single mass of data. To be able to apply analysis of variance profitably, the investigator must give careful thought to the designing of his tests to assure that the effect of the several factors to be studied are distributed as uniformly as possible throughout the testing period. Considerable knowledge of statistics as well as experience in the application of statistics to parapsychological problems is required before one may safely venture upon an investigation based upon this method. Also, caution is necessary in the interpretation of the results of analysis of variance.

The four methods mentioned thus far in this section are standard statistical procedures, and the reader who wishes further information about any of them may find it in general textbooks on statistics. The procedures now to be mentioned are, on the other hand, largely methods that were first developed to meet a need in psi research, and references will be given to the descriptions of them in the parapsychological literature.

B. Evaluation of Multiple-Calling Card Data

In testing a number of subjects at the same time, the experimenter may for convenience use only one random card order for each run and have all the subjects make their calls for the same targets. If such group results were evaluated by the methods that apply to individual test, every call would be taken as a separate trial; that is, for each target there would be as many trials as there were subjects responding to it. Actually, the only assuredly random basis for a statistical test is the *target order*, and taking each call as a trial in multiple-calling data violates the assumptions of randomness and statistical independence underlying the statistical methods. A statistically sound method for evaluating multiple-calling data has been developed.* A proper method is therefore available but one that is time-consuming to apply. The additional time required for the analysis may well amount to more than was saved at the start of the experiment by not providing a separate target order for each subject. Also, using a separate target for each call provides a more sensitive test for detecting ESP.

C. Evaluation of Verbal Material

The question of whether unrestricted verbal material contains information applying to a particular person or situation beyond what mere guessing could account for has arisen in parapsychology primarily in connection with the study of "mediumship." Such a study might be conducted, for example, by handing the subject (medium) at each session a sealed envelope containing a snapshot, and then taking a full record of the personal descrip-

---

* For the original statement and solution of the problem in general terms (the symbolic language of mathematical statistics), see Greville.[2]

tions and references given by the subject. The question is: Do the subject's remarks fit the facts associated with the snapshot to any reliable degree, or are they just as likely to be true for any photograph selected at random? The Greville method for multiple-calling data has been adapted and applied to the evaluation of verbal material. This method was described in an article which also contains a general discussion of the statistical difficulties which complicate the evaluation of verbal material and traces the steps in the development of a reliable method.[4]

D. Evaluation of Picture Tests

ESP tests have also been made with target material which allows the subject a greater freedom of response than he has in a test with a clearly defined range of targets. The type of "free material" used most frequently has been pictures cut from magazines. The subject, for example, is told only that some kind of picture has been sealed inside an opaque envelope and that he is to try to make a drawing on a blank sheet of paper to duplicate the target as closely as possible. In such a test, there is no definite probability value that can be assigned to the fact that a particular picture was selected as the target. Without a defined probability of success on each trial, the results do not lend themselves directly to statistical evaluation.

Forced matching methods have been used as a means of converting target pictures and the subject's drawings to numerical values that can be assessed. To meet the requirements of this method, the subject might be asked to make drawings for, say, four concealed target pictures. The experimenter removes the pictures from their envelopes without letting the subject know the order. The subject then ranks his four drawings against each target, assigning a value of 4 for the one that shows the closest resemblance, 3 for the second best, 2 for the third best, and 1 for the worst. After the four drawings have been matched against each of the four targets in this way, the process is repeated, with the four targets being "force matched" against each of the drawings. The matching values are combined to give a total score for each of the sixteen drawing-target correspondences, and the scores obtained in the four cases in which each drawing was compared with its real target are evaluated in relation to the expected chance values by means of Student's *t* test.

The above description covers in general terms the method referred to as *preferential matching.** Other matching methods have also been used for dealing with picture-and-drawing tests of ESP, but this one will serve as a general illustration of the principle which they all have in common: When the design of the experiment does not provide a quantitative basis as the starting point, the results must be reduced to numerical terms at a later stage by some suitable objective (and arbitrary) procedure before they can be evaluated statistically.   It is certainly more convenient to start with a quantitative test, and an experimenter would be justified in using unrestricted targets only if his research objective should require or would be better served by such material.

E. Evaluation of "Clock" Card Tests

Clock-face cards were introduced as targets for ESP tests to allow the possibility of scoring each call in terms of how far it missed the target.   Each card contains a circle with the 12 hours and with a single hand pointing to one of them.   The position of the hand varies at random from card to card and the subject simply calls an hour, attempting to hit the one shown on the concealed target.

Each call is scored in two ways: first, as a hit or a miss, as is usually done in ESP tests; secondly, in terms of how far away (to the left or right) the call is from the hour shown on the target.   The "direct hit" scores are suitable for statistical evaluation by the methods commonly used for ESP results.   For evaluating the "dispersion" score, a new statistical method was required.[6] The two methods are applied to the same data from clock cards as a basis of comparing the "amount" of ESP shown by the two ways of scoring the results.

F. The Exact Probability of a Two-by-Two Table

This method is not one developed to answer a question first raised in parapsychology, but it is frequently needed for the evaluation of a two-by-two table.   The method of testing such a table

---

* For a full explanation of the method, see Humphrey.[5]

by chi square was given on pp. 178–9. But when the observed value in one or more of the four cells is very small (say not over 3), chi square is not likely to be applicable since a X^2 value is not reliable if the *expected value* in any cell falls much below 10. The chi-square test only gives a reliably close approximation to the P value of a two-by-two distribution under the above conditions. With small observed values, it is practicable to compute the *exact probability* that the observed distribution or a more unlikely one might have occurred on a chance basis when the row and column totals do not change. If the figures in a fourfold table are

a	b
c	d

the exact probability for the observed case would be

$$P = \frac{(a+b)!(c+d)!(a+c)!(b+d)!}{(a+b+c+d)!\,a!\,b!\,c!\,d!}$$

Assume that c is the smallest number and is equal to 1. Then, to complete the analysis, obtain in the same way the probability for the only possible more extreme case in which c = 0 and the values of a, b, and d are adjusted to keep the same marginal totals, and add the two probabilities.

As an illustration, suppose that the figures in the example given on page 178 had been, instead of the ones shown there, as follows:

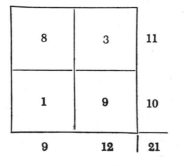

8	3	11
1	9	10
9	12	21

$$P = \frac{11!10!12!9!}{21!8!9!3!1!} = .0056$$

The only more unlikely distribution is:

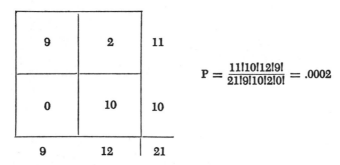

$$P = \frac{11!10!12!9!}{21!9!10!2!0!} = .0002$$

The desired P value is therefore .0056 + .0002 = .0058. The observed distribution is therefore not likely to have occurred solely on the basis of random variation, and with an equally well planned and safeguarded experiment the investigator would draw the same conclusion as was reached from the chi-square test of the previous two-by-two table.

The above illustration takes into account only one tail of the curve of frequency of fourfold tables, and the P value found is appropriate only in those instances in which the investigator predicted in advance the direction of deviation and would not have drawn any conclusion from an unusual result near the opposite end of the curve. If the probability for a given case in terms of chance occurrence at either end of the curve is desired, it is necessary to work out also the cases at the other extreme which have a chance probability of occurrence that is equal to or smaller than that of the observed case, and to add in these P values as well.

VI. Criterion of Significance

The aim of every statistical analysis is to arrive at a probability value for the results which is an indication of how frequently a result *at least as unlikely as the one found* (that is, as different as it is from chance expectation) would occur merely on a chance basis.

Every statistical analysis is literally a test of the chance hypothesis. When a low P-value has been predicted and is found

(one, say, of the order of .01 or lower), it becomes unreasonable
to suppose that only chance factors were operating. A statistical
test never completely excludes the chance explanation; it only
tells us when we are justified to *infer* that some principle was
operating consistently to influence the results and whether to
plan further investigations to test the consequences of this conclusion. The acid test of a conclusion reached on the basis of
a statistical analysis is whether investigations made to follow it
up lead to better understanding and control of the phenomena.
The justification of the use of statistics lies, therefore, in the future
of any field of research—in the steady advancement of knowledge through the judgments and predictions made on the basis
of the statistical findings.

In order for such judgments to have the necessary objectivity,
a *criterion of significance* is established by practice and general
agreement among the research workers in a particular field. To
a considerable extent the same probability level is accepted as
"significant" among the various branches of science that depend
upon statistical evaluations. Most workers in parapsychology
accept a probability of .01 as the criterion of significance. This
is not to say that there is any special magic in this value: that
chance governs any result that fails to meet this criterion, and that
some non-chance principle *must be present* when a P of .01 or
less is obtained. However, we need a precise—albeit arbitrary—
criterion of significance as a standard which can be applied in
each experiment.

The acceptance of a criterion of significance does not mean that
proof of the occurrence of any given phenomenon can be claimed
merely because a result at the .01 probability level is obtained.
Establishment of a scientific principle must always wait upon
repetition and confirmation; and the amount of confirmation required will depend upon various things, not least among them
being the question of how surprising or how unlikely a hypothesis
appears to be.

References

1. RHINE, J. B., *et al.*: *Extrasensory Perception After Sixty Years.*
New York, Holt, 1940.

2. GREVILLE, T. N. E.:   On multiple matching with one variable deck. *Ann. Math. Statistics, 15*:432–434, 1944.

3. PRATT, J. G.:   The variance for multiple-calling ESP data.   *J. Parapsychol., 18*:37–40, 1954.

4. PRATT, J. G., and BIRGE, W. R.:   Appraising verbal test material in parapsychology.   *J. Parapsychol., 12*:236–256, 1948.

5. HUMPHREY, B. M.:   *Handbook of Tests in Parapsychology.*   Durham, N. C., Parapsychology Laboratory, 1948.

6. FISK, G. W., and MITCHELL, A. M. J.:   ESP experiments with clock cards: A new technique with differential scoring.   *J. Soc. Psychical Res., 37*:1–14, 1953.

Additional Reading

BROWNLEE, K. A.:   *Industrial Experimentation.*   London, Her Majesty's Stat. Off., 1949.

COCHRAN, W. G., and COX, G. M.:   Experimental Designs.   New York, Wiley, 1956.

EDWARDS, A. L.:   *Statistical Methods for the Behavioral Sciences.*   New York, Rinehart, 1954.

FISHER, R. A., and YATES, F.:   *Statistical Tables.*   London, Oliver and Boyd, 1953.

FISHER, R. A.:   *Statistical Methods for Research Workers,* 10th Ed.   New York, Hafner, 1948.

HOEL, F. G.:   *Introduction to Mathematical Statistics.*   New York, Wiley, 1954.

RHINE, J. B., *et al.*:   *Extrasensory Perception after Sixty Years.*   New York, Holt, 1940, pp. 22–48, 349–394.

SNEDECOR, G. W.:   *Statistical Methods.*   Ames, Iowa, Collegiate Press, 1946.

WILKS, S. S.:   *Elementary Statistical Analysis.*   Princeton, N. J., Princeton, 1951.

LIBRARY ST. MARY'S COLLEGE

Tables

List of Tables

EXPLANATION: Each run consists of 25 trials, each with a 1/5 probability of success. If the score total obtained for a given number of runs falls within the limits indicated in the "Encouraging" column, the approximate odds against obtaining so large a score in a pure chance series are between 10-to-1 and 20-to-1. If the score total obtained equals or exceeds that given in the "Good" column, the odds are 100-to-1 or higher The same odds would apply to obtained score totals that are *below* the expected chance score to the same degree as those shown in the table are *above* the expected chance score.

TABLE II
RATING TABLES FOR PK TESTS FOR TARGET FACE

Number of Runs	Expected Chance Score Total	Actual Score Total Obtained	
		Encouraging	Good (Range of Statistical Significance)
4	16	23–24	26 and above
5	20	27–29	31 and above
6	24	32–33	36 and above
7	28	37–38	41 and above
8	32	41–43	46 and above
9	36	46–47	51 and above
10	40	50–52	55 and above
12	48	59–61	65 and above
14	56	68–70	74 and above
16	64	77–79	83 and above
18	72	86–88	92 and above
20	80	94–97	102 and above
25	100	116–119	124 and above
30	120	137–140	146 and above
35	140	159–162	168 and above
40	160	180–183	190 and above
45	180	201–205	212 and above
50	200	222–226	234 and above
60	240	265–269	277 and above
70	280	306–311	320 and above
80	320	348–353	363 and above
90	360	390–395	405 and above
100	400	432–437	448 and above

EXPLANATION: Each run consists of 24 trials, each with a 1/6 probability of success. If the score total obtained for a given number of runs falls within the limits indicated in the "Encouraging" column, the approximate odds against obtaining so large a score in a pure chance series are between 10-to-1 and 20-to-1. If the score total obtained equals or exceeds that given in the "Good" column, the odds are 100-to-1 or higher. The same odds would apply to obtained score totals that are *below* the expected chance score to the same degree as those shown in the table are *above* the expected chance score.

TABLE III
Rating Table for Results of PK Placement Tests

Number of Trials	Expected Chance Score Total	Actual Score Total Obtained Encouraging	Good (Range of Statistical Significance)
100	50	59–60	63 and above
120	60	70–71	75 and above
140	70	81–82	86 and above
160	80	91–93	97 and above
180	90	102–104	108 and above
200	100	113–115	119 and above
220	110	123–125	130 and above
240	120	134–136	140 and above
260	130	144–147	151 and above
280	140	155–157	162 and above
300	150	165–168	173 and above
320	160	176–178	184 and above
340	170	186–189	194 and above
360	180	197–199	205 and above
380	190	207–210	216 and above
400	200	217–220	226 and above
420	210	228–231	237 and above
440	220	238–241	248 and above
460	230	249–252	258 and above
480	240	259–262	269 and above
500	250	270–273	279 and above
600	300	321–325	332 and above
700	350	373–377	385 and above
800	400	425–429	437 and above
900	450	476–480	489 and above
1000	500	527–532	541 and above

EXPLANATION: A trial consists of an individual object which is released while the subjects concentrate upon having it stop in the "target" area instead of in the equal, non-target area. (For example, five objects released at one time count as five trials.) It is essential that each side of the throwing surface should be used as the target for the same number of trials, and that no change in or adjustment to the apparatus be made except when the trials for the two sides are equal. If the actual score total obtained (the total number of objects stopping within the target area) falls within the limits indicated in the "Encouraging" column, the approximate odds against obtaining so large a score in a pure chance series are between 10-to-1 and 20-to-1. If the score total obtained equals or exceeds that given in the "Good" column, the odds are 100-to-1 or higher. The same odds would apply to obtained score totals that are *below* the expected chance score to the same degree as those shown in the table are *above* the expected chance score.

TABLE IV
Standard Deviations for ESP Card Tests

Runs	SD	Runs	SD	Runs	SD	Runs	SD
4	4.00	29	10.77	54	14.70	79	17.78
5	4.47	30	10.95	55	14.83	80	17.89
6	4.90	31	11.14	56	14.97	81	18.00
7	5.29	32	11.31	57	15.10	82	18.11
8	5.66	33	11.49	58	15.23	83	18.22
9	6.00	34	11.66	59	15.36	84	18.33
10	6.32	35	11.83	60	15.49	85	18.44
11	6.63	36	12.00	61	15.62	86	18.55
12	6.93	37	12.17	62	15.75	87	18.65
13	7.21	38	12.33	63	15.87	88	18.76
14	7.48	39	12.49	64	16.00	89	18.87
15	7.75	40	12.65	65	16.12	90	18.97
16	8.00	41	12.81	66	16.25	91	19.08
17	8.25	42	12.96	67	16.37	92	19.18
18	8.49	43	13.11	68	16.49	93	19.29
19	8.72	44	13.27	69	16.61	94	19.39
20	8.94	45	13.42	70	16.73	95	19.49
21	9.17	46	13.56	71	16.85	96	19.60
22	9.38	47	13.71	72	16.97	97	19.70
23	9.59	48	13.86	73	17.09	98	19.80
24	9.80	49	14.00	74	17.20	99	19.90
25	10.00	50	14.14	75	17.32	100	20.00
26	10.20	51	14.28	76	17.44		
27	10.39	52	14.42	77	17.55		
28	10.58	53	14.56	78	17.66		

Explanation:. The table lists the standard deviations for ESP card tests of from 4 to 100 runs in length, each run consisting of 25 trials, each with a 1/5 probability of success. For details regarding the use of the standard deviation in evaluating the results of ESP tests, see pages 172–3.

The SD for a series longer than 100 runs may be found by *doubling* the SD value shown in the table for *one-fourth* the number of runs in the longer series. Thus the SD for 200 runs is $2 \times 14.14 = 28.28$.

TABLE V
STANDARD DEVIATIONS FOR PK TESTS FOR TARGET FACE

Runs	SD	Runs	SD*	Runs	SD	Runs	SD
4	3.65	29	9.83	54	13.42	79	16.23
5	4.08	30	10.00	55	13.54	80	16.33
6	4.47	31	10.17	56	13.66	81	16.43
7	4.83	32	10.33	57	13.78	82	16.53
8	5.16	33	10.49	58	13.90	83	16.63
9	5.48	34	10.65	59	14.02	84	16.73
10	5.77	35	10.80	60	14.14	85	16.83
11	6.06	36	10.95	61	14.26	86	16.93
12	6.32	37	11.10	62	14.38	87	17.03
13	6.58	38	11.25	63	14.49	88	17.13
14	6.83	39	11.40	64	14.61	89	17.22
15	7.07	40	11.55	65	14.72	90	17.32
16	7.30	41	11.69	66	14.83	91	17.42
17	7.53	42	11.83	67	14.94	92	17.51
18	7.75	43	11.97	68	15.06	93	17.61
19	7.96	44	12.11	69	15.17	94	17.70
20	8.16	45	12.25	70	15.27	95	17.80
21	8.37	46	12.38	71	15.38	96	17.89
22	8.56	47	12.52	72	15.49	97	17.98
23	8.76	48	12.65	73	15.60	98	18.07
24	8.94	49	12.78	74	15.71	99	18.17
25	9.13	50	12.91	75	15.81	100	18.26
26	9.31	51	13.04	76	15.92		
27	9.49	52	13.17	77	16.02		
28	9.66	53	13.29	78	16.12		

EXPLANATION: The table lists the standard deviations for PK tests of from 4 to 100 runs in length, each run consisting of 24 throws of individual dice for a target face regardless of the number of dice released at a time. For details regarding the use of the standard deviation in evaluating the results of PK tests, see page 174.

For series of more than 100 runs, the standard deviation may be found by doubling the SD shown in the table for one-fourth the given number of trials. Thus the SD of 200 runs is 2 × 12.91 = 25.82.

TABLE VI
STANDARD DEVIATIONS FOR PK PLACEMENT TESTS

Trials	SD	Trials	SD
100	5.00	560	11.83
120	5.48	580	12.04
140	5.92	600	12.25
160	6.32	620	12.45
180	6.71	640	12.65
200	7.07	660	12.85
220	7.42	680	13.04
240	7.75	700	13.23
260	8.06	720	13.42
280	8.37	740	13.60
300	8.66	760	13.78
320	8.94	780	13.96
340	9.22	800	14.14
360	9.49	820	14.32
380	9.75	840	14.49
400	10.00	860	14.66
420	10.25	880	14.83
440	10.49	900	15.00
460	10.72	920	15.17
480	10.95	940	15.33
500	11.18	960	15.49
520	11.40	980	15.65
540	11.62	1000	15.81

EXPLANATION: The table lists the standard deviations for PK placement tests of from 100 to 1000 trials, each trial consisting of the release of an individual object regardless of the number used on each attempt. For details regarding the use of the standard deviation in evaluating the results of PK placement tests, see page 174. If the number of objects used regularly for each release does not bring the total trials of the series to one of the numbers shown in the table, a different number of objects may be used for throws (equally divided between the two sides of the table as targets) to achieve the desired total number of trials. For series of more than 1000 trials, the standard deviation may be found by doubling the SD shown in the table for one-fourth the given number of trials. Thus the SD of 2000 trials is 2 × 11.18 = 22.36.

TABLE VII

PROBABILITIES OF CHANCE OCCURRENCE OF HIGH SCORES ON SINGLE ESP RUNS

Score	Probability of Occurrence of the Given Score or a Higher one
8	.109123
9	.046775
10	.017333
11	.005556
12	.001541
13	.000370
14	.000077
15	.000014
16	.000002

EXPLANATION: The table shows the theoretical probabilities based upon the binomial distribution, which applies to ESP run scores with the "open" pack, or a random distribution of targets. The theoretical probabilities are slightly different for scores based upon the "closed" pack, but the differences are ordinarily slight and the above values may be applied to scores with the closed pack without any appreciable danger of *overestimating* the significance of the run score obtained.

TABLE VIII

TABLE FOR CONVERTING CRITICAL RATIOS INTO PROBABILITY VALUES

CR	Probability	CR	Probability
1.0	.32	2.7	.0069
1.5	.13	2.8	.0051
2.0	.046	2.9	.0037
2.1	.036	3.0	.0027
2.3	.021	3.5	.00047
2.4	.016	4.0	.000063
2.5	.012	4.5	.0000068
2.6	.0093	5.0	.00000057

EXPLANATION: By locating in the table the CR value actually obtained in making a statistical analysis of results, the investigator may find the probability value which indicates how often a CR *at least this large* would be expected to occur purely on a chance basis. For example, a CR of 2.6 or larger would be found solely on the basis of chance variation less than one time in 100 attempts, on the average. In a properly designed and executed psi experiment, a CR of 2.6 or higher is rated as statistically significant.

The probabilities listed apply to CR's based upon either positive or negative deviations. (For further details on the use and interpretation of the table, see Chapter 9.)

LIBRARY ST. MARY'S COLLEGE

TABLE IX

Theoretical Binominal Distribution of ESP Run Scores and its Application in a Chi-square Goodness of Fit Test

Run Score	Binomial Probability	Application to a 200-Run Series			
		Expected (E)		Observed (O)	$X^2 \left(= \dfrac{(O-E)^2}{E} \right)$
0	.003778	.76 } 5.48		2 } 7	.42
1	.023612	4.72		5	
2	.070835	14.17		18	1.03
3	.135768	27.15		25	.17
4	.186681	37.34		30	1.44
5	.196015	39.20		27	3.80
6	.163346	32.67		26	1.36
7	.110842	22.17		31	3.52
8	.062348	12.47		21	5.83
9	.029442	5.89		10	
10	.011777	2.35		1	
11	.004015	.80		2	
12	.001171	.23		1	
13	.000293	.06		0	
14	.000063	.01		1	
15	.000012	.00		0	
16	.000002	.00		0	
17	.000000	.00 } 9.34		0 } 15	3.43
18	.000000	.00		0	
19	.000000	.00		0	
20	.000000	.00		0	
21	.000000	.00		0	
22	.000000	.00		0	
23	.000000	.00		0	
24	.000000	.00		0	
25	.000000	.00		0	
	1.000,000	199.99		200	$X^2 = 21.00$

Degrees of freedom = 8, P = .0071

Explanation: The first column gives the 26 possible scores on a run through the regular ESP pack. The second column shows the relative chance frequency of occurrence of each score for a random or "open" order of 25 symbols; these values are the 26 terms of the binomial expansion, $(.2 + .8)^{25}$. (The distribution for the. balanced or "closed" pack differs slightly from the binomial but the difference is so slight that it can usually be ignored in practice.) The third column shows the expected chance frequency of scores in a 200-run series. The fourth column lists a frequency of "obtained" scores in an assumed series of 200 runs. The fifth column gives the values of chi square for the different scores, with those at the two extremes of the distribution being grouped so that no X^2 will be based on an expected value of less than 5 (and preferably not below 10). The sum of the chi squares (21.00 in this instance) may be looked up in Table X and the corresponding probability value can then be read in the appropriate column for the degrees of freedom involved in the analysis. (For a goodness-of-fit test, the degrees of freedom are one less than the number of individual chi-square categories.)

TABLE X   199
Elderton's Chi Square Tables

χ^2	$n'=3$	$n'=4$	$n'=5$	$n'=6$	$n'=7$	$n'=8$	$n'=9$	$n'=10$	$n'=11$
1	·606531	·801253	·909796	·962566	·985612	·994829	·998249	·999438	·999828
2	·367879	·572407	·735759	·849146	·919699	·959840	·981012	·991468	·996340
3	·223130	·391625	·557825	·699986	·808847	·885002	·934357	·964295	·981424
4	·135335	·261464	·406006	·549416	·676676	·779778	·857123	·911413	·947347
5	·082085	·171797	·287298	·415880	·543813	·659963	·757576	·834308	·891178
6	·049787	·111610	·199148	·306219	·423190	·539750	·647232	·739919	·815263
7	·030197	·071897	·135888	·220640	·320847	·428880	·536632	·637119	·725444
8	·018316	·046012	·091578	·156236	·238103	·332594	·433470	·534146	·628837
9	·011109	·029291	·061099	·109064	·173578	·252656	·342296	·437274	·532104
10	·006738	·018566	·040428	·075235	·124652	·188573	·265026	·350485	·440493
11	·004087	·011726	·026564	·051380	·088376	·138619	·201699	·275709	·357518
12	·002479	·007383	·017351	·034787	·061969	·100558	·151204	·213308	·285057
13	·001503	·004637	·011276	·023379	·043036	·072109	·111850	·162607	·223672
14	·000912	·002905	·007295	·015609	·029636	·051181	·081765	·122325	·172992
15	·000553	·001817	·004701	·010363	·020256	·036000	·059145	·090937	·132061
16	·000335	·001134	·003019	·006844	·013754	·025116	·042380	·066881	·099632
17	·000203	·000707	·001933	·004500	·009283	·017396	·030109	·048716	·074364
18	·000123	·000440	·001234	·002947	·006232	·011970	·021226	·035174	·054964
19	·000075	·000273	·000786	·001922	·004164	·008187	·014860	·025193	·040263
20	·000045	·000170	·000499	·001250	·002769	·005570	·010336	·017913	·029253
21	·000028	·000105	·000317	·000810	·001835	·003770	·007147	·012650	·021093
22	·000017	·000065	·000200	·000524	·001211	·002541	·004916	·008880	·015105
23	·000010	·000040	·000127	·000338	·000796	·001705	·003364	·006197	·010747
24	·000006	·000025	·000080	·000217	·000522	·001139	·002292	·004301	·007600
25	·000004	·000016	·000050	·000139	·000341	·000759	·001554	·002971	·005345
26	·000002	·000010	·000032	·000090	·000223	·000504	·001050	·002043	·003740
27	·000001	·000006	·000020	·000057	·000145	·000333	·000707	·001399	·002604
28	·000001	·000004	·000012	·000037	·000094	·000220	·000474	·000954	·001805
29	·000001	·000002	·000008	·000023	·000061	·000145	·000317	·000648	·001246
30	·000000	·000001	·000005	·000015	·000039	·000095	·000211	·000439	·000857
40	·000000	·000000	·000000	·000000	·000001	·000001	·000003	·000008	·000017
50	·000000	·000000	·000000	·000000	·000000	·000000	·000000	·000000	·000000
60	·000000	·000000	·000000	·000000	·000000	·000000	·000000	·000000	·000000
70	·000000	·000000	·000000	·000000	·000000	·000000	·000000	·000000	·000000

Explanation: In these chi square tables, n' equals degrees of freedom, n, plus one. The entries give the probability of a chi square greater than or equal to the tabular value, for the corresponding degrees of freedom. For values of n' greater than 30, chi square may be interpreted by converting it to a critical ratio by the formula: $C.R. = \sqrt{2X^2} - \sqrt{2n-1}$.

We wish to express our thanks to the editors of *Biometrika* for their kind permission to reproduce Elderton's Chi Square Tables from Pearson's *Tables for Statisticians and Biometricians*.

TABLE X—*Continued*   200
ELDERTON'S CHI SQUARE TABLES

χ^2	$n'=12$	$n'=13$	$n'=14$	$n'=15$	$n'=16$	$n'=17$	$n'=18$	$n'=19$	$n'=20$
1	·999950	·999986	·999997	·999999	1·	1·	1·	1·	1·
2	·998496	·999406	·999774	·999917	·999970	·999990	·999997	·999999	1·
3	·990726	·995544	·997934	·999074	·999598	·999830	·999931	·999972	·999989
4	·969917	·983436	·991191	·995466	·997737	·998903	·999483	·999763	·999894
5	·931167	·957979	·975193	·985813	·992127	·995754	·997771	·998860	·999431
6	·873365	·916082	·946153	·966491	·979749	·988095	·993187	·996197	·997929
7	·799073	·857613	·902151	·934711	·957650	·973260	·983549	·990125	·994213
8	·713304	·785131	·843601	·889327	·923783	·948867	·966547	·978637	·986671
9	·621892	·702931	·772943	·831051	·877517	·913414	·940261	·959743	·973479
10	·530387	·615960	·693934	·762183	·819739	·866628	·903610	·931906	·952946
11	·443263	·528919	·610817	·686036	·752594	·809485	·856564	·894357	·923839
12	·362642	·445680	·527643	·606303	·679028	·743980	·800136	·847237	·885624
13	·293326	·369041	·447812	·526524	·602298	·672758	·736186	·791573	·838571
14	·232993	·300708	·373844	·449711	·525529	·598714	·667102	·729091	·783691
15	·182498	·241436	·307354	·378154	·451418	·524638	·595482	·661967	·722598
16	·141130	·191236	·249129	·313374	·382051	·452961	·523834	·592547	·657277
17	·107876	·149597	·199304	·256178	·318864	·385597	·454366	·523105	·589868
18	·081581	·115691	·157520	·206781	·262666	·323897	·388841	·455653	·522438
19	·061094	·088529	·123104	·164949	·213734	·268663	·328532	·391823	·456836
20	·045341	·067086	·095210	·130141	·171932	·220220	·274229	·332819	·394578
21	·033371	·050380	·072929	·101632	·136830	·178510	·226291	·279413	·336801
22	·024374	·037520	·055362	·078614	·107804	·143191	·184719	·231985	·284256
23	·017676	·027726	·041677	·060270	·084140	·113735	·149251	·190590	·237342
24	·012733	·020341	·031130	·045822	·065093	·089504	·119435	·155028	·196152
25	·009117	·014822	·023084	·034566	·049943	·069824	·094710	·124915	·160542
26	·006490	·010734	·017001	·025887	·038023	·054028	·074461	·099758	·130189
27	·004595	·007727	·012441	·019254	·028736	·041483	·058068	·078995	·104653
28	·003238	·005532	·009050	·014228	·021569	·031620	·044938	·062055	·083428
29	·002270	·003940	·006546	·010450	·016085	·023936	·034526	·048379	·065985
30	·001585	·002792	·004710	·007632	·011921	·018002	·026345	·037446	·051798
40	·000036	·000072	·000138	·000255	·000453	·000778	·001294	·002087	·003272
50	·000001	·000001	·000003	·000006	·000012	·000023	·000042	·000075	·000131
60	·000000	·000000	·000000	·000000	·000000	·000001	·000001	·000002	·000004
70	·000000	·000000	·000000	·000000	·000000	·000000	·000000	·000000	·000000

TABLE X—*Continued*
ELDERTON'S CHI SQUARE TABLES

χ^2	$n'=21$	$n'=22$	$n'=23$	$n'=24$	$n'=25$	$n'=26$	$n'=27$	$n'=28$	$n'=29$	$n'=30$
1	1·	1·	1·	1·	1·	1·	1·	1·	1·	1·
2	1·	1·	1·	1·	1·	1·	1·	1·	1·	1·
3	·999996	·999998	·999999	1·	1·	1·	1·	1·	1·	1·
4	·999954	·999980	·999992	·999997	·999999	1·	1·	1·	1·	1·
5	·999722	·999868	·999939	·999972	·999987	·999994	·999998	·999999	1·	1·
6	·998898	·999427	·999708	·999855	·999929	·999966	·999984	·999993	·999997	·999999
7	·996685	·998142	·998980	·999452	·999711	·999851	·999924	·999962	·999981	·999991
8	·991868	·995143	·997160	·998371	·999085	·999494	·999726	·999853	·999924	·999960
9	·982907	·989214	·993331	·995957	·997595	·998596	·999194	·999546	·999748	·999863
10	·968171	·978912	·986304	·991277	·994547	·996653	·997981	·998803	·999302	·999599
11	·946223	·962787	·974749	·983189	·989012	·992946	·995549	·997239	·998315	·998988
12	·916076	·939617	·957379	·970470	·979908	·986567	·991173	·994294	·996372	·997728
13	·877384	·908624	·933161	·951990	·966121	·976501	·983974	·989247	·992900	·995384
14	·830496	·869599	·901479	·926871	·946650	·961732	·973000	·981254	·987189	·991377
15	·776408	·822952	·862238	·894634	·920759	·941383	·957334	·969432	·978436	·985015
16	·716624	·769650	·815886	·855268	·888076	·914828	·936203	·952947	·965819	·975536
17	·652974	·711106	·763362	·809251	·848662	·881793	·909083	·931122	·948589	·962181
18	·587408	·649004	·705988	·757489	·803008	·842390	·875773	·903519	·926149	·944272
19	·521826	·585140	·645328	·701224	·751990	·797120	·836430	·870001	·898136	·921288
20	·457930	·521261	·583040	·641912	·696776	·746825	·791556	·830756	·864464	·892927
21	·397132	·458944	·520738	·581087	·638725	·692609	·741964	·786288	·825349	·859149
22	·340511	·399510	·459889	·520252	·579267	·635744	·688697	·737377	·781291	·820189
23	·288795	·343979	·401730	·460771	·519798	·577564	·632947	·685013	·733041	·776543
24	·242392	·293058	·347229	·403808	·461597	·519373	·575965	·630316	·681535	·728932
25	·201431	·247164	·297075	·350285	405760	·462373	·518975	·574462	·627835	·678248
26	·165812	·206449	·251682	·300866	·353165	·407598	·463105	·518600	·573045	·625491
27	·135264	·170853	·211226	·255967	·304453	·355884	·409333	·463794	·518247	·571705
28	·109399	·140151	·175681	·215781	·260040	·307853	·358458	·410973	·464447	·517913
29	·087759	·114002	·144861	·180310	·220131	·263916	·311082	·360899	·412528	·465066
30	·069854	·091988	·118464	·149402	·184752	·224289	·267611	·314154	·363218	·414004
40	·004995	·007437	·010812	·015369	·021387	·029164	·039012	·051237	·066128	·083937
50	·000221	·000365	·000586	·000921	·001416	·002131	·003144	·004551	·006467	·009032
60	·000007	·000013	·000022	·000038	·000064	·000104	·000168	·000264	·000407	·000618
70	·000000	·000000	·000001	·000001	·000002	·000004	·000007	·000011	·000019	·000030

Some Significant Events in Parapsychology

Some Significant Events in the Development
of Parapsychology

Until the history of parapsychology is written, students approaching the field will find it difficult to acquire a conception of the developmental chronology of this branch of science. It will be of some assistance to him, however, merely to have a listing of some of the more significant events and especially to know the starting points of developments that have proved to be important. Among the events that seem most outstanding in today's retrospect are: (1) Those steps that first called scientific attention to the existence of a body of phenomena awaiting exploration. (2) Main beginnings on the scientific investigation of parapsychical phenomena. (3) New problem areas opened up for research in the field. (4) The coming in of support for research and other signs of growing recognition that indicate the progress the science has made over the years. The list that follows is, of course, an arbitrary selection that may at best only serve as an introductory tracing of outlines of the growth of this new branch.

1871 Report of the Dialectical Society of London on parapsychical claims, especially those associated with mediumship.

1876 Prof. William Barrett's paper at the meetings of the British Association for the Advancement of Science at Glasgow on the identification of cards at a distance by a hypnotized subject.

1882 The founding of the Society for Psychical Research.

1884 Introduction of statistical methods in parapsychology. Prof. Charles Richet applied them to data from ESP tests.

1884 The founding of the American Society for Psychical Research. This later merged with the Society for Psychical Research and still later became independent again.

1893 The doctor's degree in medicine awarded by the University of Montpellier to Albert Coste for a parapsychological thesis.

LIBRARY ST. MARY'S COLLEGE

1911   An endowed laboratory for psychical research established at Stanford University.

1912   Establishment of the Hodgson Fund at Harvard for the investigation of psychical phenomena.

1917   Publication of an experimental investigation of extrasensory perception conducted in a university department of psychology, by Dr. John E. Coover of Stanford University.

1921   First International Congress of Psychical Research, Copenhagen.

1924   The Boston Society for Psychic Research founded under the leadership of Dr. Walter Franklin Prince.

1927   Research in parapsychology started at Duke under Prof. William McDougall in the Department of Psychology. The Parapsychology Laboratory established in 1934.

1933   Ph.D. degrees for research in parapsychology awarded to John F. Thomas (Duke University), Hans Bender (Bonn University), and W. H. C. Tenhaeff (University of Utrecht).

1934   Publication of the monograph, *Extrasensory Perception*, by J. B. Rhine, introduced standardized card tests for the investigation of ESP.

1935   Establishment of the Walter Franklin Prince Memorial Fellowships,for research in parapsychology at Duke.

1937   *The Journal of Parapsychology* founded under the aegis of the Duke University Press.

1937   First handbook of test procedures in parapsychology, by C. E. Stuart and J. G. Pratt.

1937   Pronouncement of the President of the Institute of Mathematical Statistics, approving the methods of statistical evaluation in parapsychology.

1937   Symposium on parapsychology held by the Aristotelian Society and Mind Association in Great Britain.

1938   Roundtable on methods in parapsychology held by the American Psychological Association at Columbus, Ohio.

1938   First report of experiments in precognition, begun in 1933 at the Parapsychology Laboratory at Duke University.

1940   Perrott Studentship in Psychical Research established at the University of Cambridge.

1940   Publication of *Extrasensory Perception After Sixty Years,* a critical survey and examination of the evidence of ESP, by five staff members of the Parapsychology Laboratory at Duke University.

1943   Report of experiments in psychokinesis begun in the Duke Laboratory in 1934.

1950   Grant by the Rockefeller Foundation to Duke for research in the Parapsychology Laboratory.

1950   The British Society of Experimental Biologists symposium in London on parapsychology.

1950   The Royal Society of Medicine (Section on Psychiatry) sponsored an address on the subject of parapsychology in London by J. B. Rhine.

1951   First Fulbright Scholar to receive a travel grant in parapsychology. Dr. S. G. Soal of London University visited Duke.

1951   The Royal Institution of Great Britain held a discourse presented by Robert H. Thouless on research in parapsychology.

1953   The Parapsychology Laboratory of Duke University received a grant from the Office of Naval Research for the investigation of ESP in animals.

1953   The University of Pittsburgh received a grant from the A. W. Mellon Educational and Charitable Trust for research in parapsychology in the Department of Physics.

1953   A professorship of parapsychology under Dr. W. H. C. Tenhaeff was established at the University of Utrecht.

1953   An international Congress of Parapsychology was held at the University of Utrecht under the sponsorship of the Parapsychology Foundation of New York, the University, and the Minister of Education of The Netherlands.

1954   The American Philosophical Association, Eastern Division, held a symposium on parapsychology.

1955   The Ciba Foundation of London held a symposium on extrasensory perception.

1955   The Ralph Drake Perry Research Fellowships in Parapsychology were established at Duke.

1956   St. Joseph's College of Philadelphia and Wayland College
        of Plainview, Texas, each established a Parapsychology
        Laboratory.

1957   The Parapsychological Association, a professional society of
        research workers in that field, was founded on June 19.

1957   The William McDougall Award ($1000) for Distinguished
        Work in Parapsychology was established on June 22 by the
        Parapsychology Laboratory at Duke.

1960   The Parapsychology Scholarship Fund established at Duke
        University. Open to qualified, interested students anywhere.

1960   A symposium on parapsychology held by the Canadian
        Physiological Society at Winnipeg.

1961   Founding of the Psychical Research Foundation at Durham,
        N. C., for research on the problem of post-mortem survival.

1961   University of King's College, Halifax, authorized opening of
        a Parapsychology Laboratory.

1961   The Ittleson Family Foundation made a grant to The Men-
        ninger Foundation for research on "creativeness and the
        paranormal."

1961   The Psychology Department of the City College of New
        York announced the establishment of graduate fellowships
        for research in parapsychology leading to the Master's de-
        gree in psychology.

1962   The Foundation for Research on the Nature of Man was
        established at Durham, N. C. The first unit of the Founda-
        tion is The McDougall Fund for Parapsychology.

Glossary

Glossary

Agent: Sender in tests for telepathy, the person whose mental states are to be apprehended by the percipient. In GESP tests, the person who looks at the stimulus object.

Average Score: Average number of hits per run.

BM (Blind Matching): An ESP card test in which the subject, holding the cards face down, sorts them into five piles, attempting to match concealed key cards (see page 148).

BT (Basic Technique): The clairvoyance technique in which each card is laid aside by the experimenter as it is called by the subject. The check-up is made at the end of the run.

Call: The ESP symbol selected by the subject in trying to identify a target.

Chance: The complex of undefined causal factors irrelevant to the purpose at hand.

Chance Expectation = Mean Chance Expectation: The most likely score if only chance variation is present.

Chance Average: Mean chance expectation expressed as an expected score, generally in terms of average per run.

Chi Square: A sum of quantities each of which is a deviation squared divided by an expected value. Also a sum of the squares of CR's.

Clairvoyance: Extrasensory perception of objective events as distinguished from telepathic perception of the mental state of another person.

CR (Critical Ratio): A measure to determine whether or not the observed deviation is significantly greater than the expected random fluctuation about the average. The CR is obtained by dividing the observed deviation by the standard deviation. (The probability of a given CR may be obtained by consulting tables of the probability integral, such as Table VIII.)

Deviation: The amount an observed number of hits or an average score varies from the mean chance expectation or chance average. A deviation may be total (for a series of runs) or average (per run).

Displacement: ESP responses to targets other than those for which the calls were intended.

211

Backward Displacement: ESP responses to targets preceding the assigned targets (the ones for which they were intended). Displacement to the targets one, two, three, etc. places preceding the assigned target are designated as (-1), (-2), (-3), etc.

Forward Displacement: ESP responses to targets coming later than the assigned targets. Displacement to the targets one, two, three, etc. places after the assigned target are designated as $(+1)$, $(+2)$, $(+3)$, etc.

DT (Down Through): The clairvoyance technique in which the cards are called down through the deck before any are removed or checked.

ESP (Extrasensory Perception): Awareness of or response to an external event or influence not apprehended by sensory means.

ESP Cards: Cards, each bearing one of the following five symbols: star, circle, three parallel wavy lines (called "waves"), square, plus.

ESP Pack: Twenty-five ESP cards.

Closed Pack: An ESP deck composed of five each of the five symbols.

Open Pack: An ESP deck made up of the ESP symbols selected in random order.

Expectation: see **Chance.**

Extrachance: Not due to chance alone.

Free Material: The stimulus objects of experiments in which an unlimited or unspecified range of stimulus objects is employed (as contrasted with methods such as card-calling in which the subject knows that the stimulus object is one of a known range).

GESP (General Extrasensory Perception): A technique designed to test the occurrence of extrasensory perception, permitting either telepathy or clairvoyance or both to operate.

High-Dice Test: A PK technique in which the aim of the subject is to try to influence a pair of dice to fall with the two upper faces totaling eight or more.

Low-Dice Test: A PK technique in which the aim of the subject is to try to influence a pair of dice to fall with the two upper faces totaling six or less.

MCE (Mean Chance Expectation): see **Chance.**

P (Probability): A mathematical estimate of the expected relative frequency of a given event if chance alone were operative.

Parapsychology: A division of psychology dealing with behavioral or personal effects that are demonstrably nonphysical (that is, which do not fall within the scope of physical principles).

Percipient = Subject: The person who makes the calls in an ESP test.

PK (Psychokinesis): The direct influence exerted on a physical system by a subject without any known intermediate physical energy or instrumentation.

Precognition: Cognition of a future event which could not be known through rational inference.

Preferential Matching: A method of scoring free responses. A judge ranks the stimulus objects (usually in sets of four) with respect to their similarity to, or association with, each response; and/or he ranks the responses with respect to their similarity to, or association with, each stimulus object.

Psi: A general term to identify personal factors or processes which are nonphysical in nature. It approximates the popular use of the word "psychic" and the technical one, "parapsychical."

Psi-Missing: Exercise of psi ability in a way that avoids the target the subject is attempting to hit.

Psi Phenomena: Occurrences which result from the operation of psi. They include the phenomena of both ESP (including precognition) and PK.

Psychical Research: Older term used for parapsychology.

QD (Quarter Distribution): The distribution of hits in the record page (or in a logical subdivision thereof, such as the set or the half-set) as found in the four equal quarters formed by dividing the selected unit horizontally and vertically.

Random Order: An order of events which displays no trends or regularities that would allow any inference regarding one event from one or more of the others in the series.

Run: A group of trials, usually the successive calling of a deck of 25 ESP cards or symbols. In PK tests, 24 single die throws regardless of the number of dice thrown at the same time.

Score: The number of hits made in one run.

Total Score: Total of scores made in a given number of runs.

Average Score: Total score divided by number of runs.

SD (Standard Deviation): Usually the theoretical root mean square of the deviations. It is obtained from the formula $\sqrt{npq}$ in which n is the number of single trials, p the probability of success per trial, and q the probability of failure.

Series: Several runs or experimental sessions that are grouped in accordance with a stated principle.

Session: A unit of an ESP or PK experiment comprising all the trials of one test occasion.

Set: A subdivision of the record page serving as a scoring unit for a consecutive group of trials, usually for the same target.

Significance: A numerical result is significant when it equals or surpasses some criterion of degree of chance improbability. The criterion commonly used in parapsychology today is a probability value of .01 or less, or a deviation in either direction such that the CR is 2.58 or greater.

Singles Test: A PK technique in which the aim of the subject is to try to influence dice to fall with a specified face up.

Spontaneous Psi Experience: Natural, unplanned occurrence of an event or experience that seems to involve parapsychial ability.

Stimulus Object: The ESP card or drawing or other object, some identifying characteristic of which is to be apprehended by the percipient.

STM (Screened Touch Matching): An ESP card test in which the subject indicates in each trial (by pointing to one of five key positions) what he thinks the top card is in the inverted pack held by the experimenter behind a screen. The card is then laid opposite that position (see page 160).

Subject: The person who is experimented upon. In ESP tests, most commonly the percipient (though also the agent in GESP and telepathy). In PK tests, any individual whose task it is to influence the objects thrown.

Target: In clairvoyance or precognition tests the stimulus object; in telepathy, the mental state of the agent. In PK tests, the faces of the die which the subject attempts to bring up in the act of throwing.

Target Card: The card which the percipient is attempting to perceive (i.e., to identify or otherwise indicate a knowledge of).

Target Pack: The deck of cards the order of which the subject is attempting to identify.

Target Face: The face on the die which the subject tries to turn up as a consequence of direct mental action.

Telepathy: Extrasensory perception of the mental activities of another person. It does not include the clairvoyant perception of objective events.

Trial: In ESP tests, a single attempt to identify a stimulus object. In PK tests, a single throw of the dice or other objects thrown.

Name Index

Subject Index

217